The Destiny of the Species

The Destiny of the Species

Man and the Future that Pulls Him

Jason J. Stellman

RESOURCE *Publications* • Eugene, Oregon

THE DESTINY OF THE SPECIES
Man and the Future that Pulls Him

Copyright © 2013 Jason J. Stellman. All rights reserved. Except for brief quotations in critical publications or reviews, no part of this book may be reproduced in any manner without prior written permission from the publisher. Write: Permissions, Wipf and Stock Publishers, 199 W. 8th Ave., Suite 3, Eugene, OR 97401.

Resource Publications
An Imprint of Wipf and Stock Publishers
199 W. 8th Ave., Suite 3
Eugene, OR 97401
www.wipfandstock.com

ISBN 13: 978-1-62032-472-1

Manufactured in the U.S.A.

This book is dedicated to all those, living and dead, who have helped instill in me a longing for the heavenly realities of which the stuff of earth are but shadows.

Contents

Acknowledgements ix

Introduction xi

1. Pushed or Pulled? 1
2. The Jagged Little Red Pill 12
3. Which Came Last, the Chicken or the Egg? 24
4. The Unmerry Merry-Go-Round 35
5. The Earthly Ties That Bind 46
6. Sin (Yes, That Word Still Exists) 56
7. From Eternity to Here 70
8. The World's Unworthiness 82
9. Divine Conflict Resolution 93
10. Apocalypse Eventually 103

Bibliography 115

Acknowledgements

I WOULD LIKE TO express my gratitude to those who were instrumental in bringing this book to fruition (whether directly or indirectly): Many thanks to everyone at Wipf and Stock Publications for their role in taking *The Destiny of the Species* from a mere idea in my head to something that others can hold in their hands; heartfelt love to my beautiful wife and children for their encouragement, prayers, and unconditional love; many thanks to the faculty of Westminster Seminary California for helping me understand what "eschatology is prior to soteriology" means; to Dale Ahlquist and David Fagerberg for their books on G.K. Chesterton which helped me to prize more highly his heavenly and elvish perspective on the wonders of the here and now; to Scott Hahn and Mark Shea for their friendship and encouragement; to the families of the church I used to pastor, Exile Presbyterian, for showing me much more grace than I ever deserved; to the readers of Creed Code Cult for always holding my feet to the fire and making me work for every biblical or theological point I try to make; to Christian Kingery for forcing me to think hard about God before bringing Him up, and for never failing to acknowledge the good points I make as well as rolling his eyes at the lame ones; and thanks lastly to my brother, Justin, who despite having provided virtually no inspiration whatsoever for this book, has reminded me several times that I neglected to acknowledge him in my last one.

Introduction

MY FIRST SERIOUS EXPOSURE to real, lived-out Christianity came during my junior year of high school. I had recently begun attending Calvary Chapel High in southern California where Monday morning chapels were mandatory. I think I slept through the first dozen or so. But during a rare moment of lucidity I inadvertently heard the youth pastor explaining Paul's words in Acts 20:22–24 (and I'll quote it in the New King James since this is the translation in which I first heard these words).

> "And see, now I go bound in the spirit to Jerusalem, not knowing the things that will happen to me there, except that the Holy Spirit testifies in every city, saying that chains and tribulations await me. But none of these things move me; nor do I count my life dear to myself, so that I may finish my race with joy, and the ministry which I received from the Lord Jesus, to testify to the gospel of the grace of God."

Of his coming trials, which were significant to say the least, the apostle says with an air of dismissal, "None of these things move me." Why? Because, he continues, "I do not count my life dear to myself." For some reason this short passage grabbed my attention and refused to let go. In fact, it still hasn't.

Another biblical passage that struck me in a powerful way in my early faith was Hebrews 11:13, and in particular a short phrase at the end of it describing the patriarchs:

> These all died in faith, not having received the promises, but having seen them afar off were assured of them, embraced them and confessed that *they were strangers and pilgrims on the earth*" (emphasis added).

Introduction

Like the passage in Acts 20, this little phrase about Abraham, Isaac, and Jacob—that they were strangers and pilgrims on the earth—presented an idea to my mind and heart that I still haven't been able to shake. Since that time I have been trying, in whatever Christian contexts I have found myself, to come to grips with and then communicate to others this idea that (to paraphrase Paul) the eternal, heavenly pleasures of the age to come make whatever this present life has to offer seem paltry and worthless in comparison. In a word, this book is but the latest attempt in an ongoing project that I expect will nag me as being ever incomplete for the duration of my earthly days.

A quick word concerning the intended audience for *The Destiny of the Species*: The reader will note that there is very little here by way of presupposed biblical or theological knowledge (especially in the early chapters). The reason for this is that this book is not intended merely for those who already have a strong grasp of the Christian faith (although it will hopefully bless and challenge them as well). Rather, this book is intended to be sufficiently simple to be understood by nonbelievers, sufficiently broad to be helpful to believers of varying backgrounds and theological traditions, and sufficiently culturally engaging to be enjoyable to all who happen to pick it up.

Jason J. Stellman
Woodinville, WA

1

Pushed or Pulled?

THERE IS A BEAUTIFUL irony in the fact that our nation's children are taught in school that they are nothing more than highly-evolved animals, and yet when little Johnny leaves the classroom and behaves accordingly, we conclude that his real problem is a lack of education. When we realize the complete consistency between (1) the belief that one is an animal and (2) barbaric, animalistic behavior, we either need to disallow the belief or allow the barbarism. What we can't do, though, is *tsk-tsk* the logical result of a worldview, particularly if it's one that we ourselves share. Hence our cultural tension—we want intellectual freedom from the confines of the religious mythology of a by-gone era, while at the same time waxing nostalgic while watching *Leave It to Beaver*. No, we don't want to return to the sterile domesticity that Ward and June inhabited, but hearing Wally and The Beave call their parents "Sir" or "Ma'am" sounds pretty nice, particularly after watching *South Park*.

As I write, it is roughly 150 years since Charles Darwin's famous book *The Origin of Species* was published. Since that time, men and women have felt a keen sense of camaraderie with the past. If we desire to know who we are in the present, we must know something about our heritage, our ancestry, our pedigree. "We know where we're going," sang Bob Marley and the Wailers, because "we know where we're from." Now, there certainly is an element of truth in the claim that, "In this bright future, we can't forget the past," but such sentiment fails to tell the whole story.

"And which 'story' is that?" you may be asking. Well, the story of mankind, of course. Your story and mine.

The Destiny of the Species

The reason that Darwin ultimately fails us is because he doesn't scratch where we truly itch. Sure, knowing about our origins is important, but the reason this question falls short is that deep down we know that, whatever we are, it has to be more than what Darwinism teaches us. Despite the flawed-yet-noble character of humanity (what Francis Schaeffer called "the mannishness of man"), it may be comforting, sometimes anyway, to delude ourselves into thinking that we really are mere animals driven by the instinct to survive and have our needs met at all costs. After all, in our cutthroat culture in which might often makes right, why not abandon all social graces and just give expression to the underbelly of our baser selves? If casualties ensue while we climb the ladder of power, if some collateral damage occurs as we seek to fulfill our own desires, if my wife gets hurt when she finds out about my mistress, so what? I mean, we're just animals, right?

Wrong. Despite the occasional bit of comfort such a theory of origins may offer, and despite the hook off of which it seems to let us, we humans just can't seem to escape the nagging feeling that life, at the end of the day, is not completely pointless. Sure, we can fool ourselves with clichés such as "Eat, drink, and be merry, for tomorrow we die," but the thought of death inevitably causes one to question the morality of his merriment. In a word, beneath the surface we all know that "You only live once" is bad news rather than good, and that what happens in Vegas doesn't stay there.

My aim in this chapter is to argue that man is distinct from the animals precisely because he is not pushed but *pulled*, he is not driven but *drawn*. The origin of the species may be descriptive, but it cannot be definitive. Give a man a glorious pedigree and nothing to live for, and the result will be despair. But take a man with a sordid past and give him hope, or even something for which to long, and his past and present will be eclipsed by his future.

Mimicry of the Maker

According to Christian theology as outlined in the pages of the Bible, man is the result of God's creative power. The first four words in most English Bibles are "In the beginning, God . . ." (It's only two in the original Hebrew.) Setting aside what I consider to be secondary issues such as what role, if any, evolution played in the process of man's development and how long ago such things took place, the fact remains that Christianity has taught for

2000 years (and Judaism for way longer) that man is no accidental result of random happenstance or natural selection. Rather, man and woman were created in the image of the God who made them. As such, we share some of God's traits and reflect—however poorly at times—his image.

One of the ways man mirrors the image of his Maker is by his longing for eternal life. Again setting aside some ancillary and technical questions, the book of Genesis (which means "Origin") teaches that God labored creatively for six days, during which time he made the heavens, the earth, the animal kingdom, and man himself. Of the seventh day we read: "Thus the heavens and the earth were finished, and all the host of them. And on the seventh day God finished his work that he had done, and he rested on the seventh day from all his work that he had done. So God blessed the seventh day and made it holy, because on it God rested from all his work that he had done in creation" (Gen. 2:1–3). Lest we imagine that God's "rest" on the seventh day was due to fatigue from manual labor, we would do well to call to mind the fact that "the everlasting God, the Creator of the ends of the earth, neither faints nor grows weary" (Isa. 40:28). No, God's rest on the seventh day consisted of nothing less than his enjoyment of his own creative work, with the seventh day marking the beginning (if we may so speak) of Sabbath bliss.

The point of God's entering into Sabbath rest was not to add one more thing to the list of eternal blessings he enjoys, but to share that eternal and blessed rest with us. As I mentioned before, man's task was to be a divine image-bearer, to mimic the God who made him. If God labored and then rested, therefore, man was to labor and then rest. If God sat blissfully and eternally enthroned, then such would be the destiny of man the imager of God.

Hardwired for Heaven

To put this another way, if all human beings are created in the image of God, then it follows that all human beings are hardwired for heaven. We are, by our very nature, future-oriented with a built-in longing for eternal life.

The question can legitimately be asked, "But how do we know that heaven even exists in the first place? How can we be certain that there is such a thing as 'eternal life'?" Ironically enough, the question is answered in the asking, for the very fact that man has always longed for the afterlife is itself strong evidence that there actually is such a thing. Peter Kreeft writes, "Innate desires bespeak real objects. If there is hunger, there is food. And there is an innate hunger for eternity." He continues: "But this food is not found under the sun. . . . It is Yonder. There is more. There are more things in Heaven and earth than are dreamed of in all our philosophies. That is the announcement of hope. Hope's messenger has infiltrated even into the castle of doom. Our desire for eternity, our divine discontent with time, is hope's messenger."[1] C.S. Lewis made a similar point, "If I find in myself a desire which no experience in this world can satisfy, the most probably explanation is that I was made for another world."[2] Modern man's atheism is a relatively new phenomenon, one peculiar to the industrialized West. The vast majority of people throughout history have recognized themselves as the spiritual beings that God made them to be (whether they acknowledge the one true God or not). Try as we might to drown out the divine Voice amid the dull din of our daily distractions, we simply cannot ignore forever the truth that screams at us from all sides, demanding our attention: God made us, and the "discontent" we feel is indeed a divine one, strategically placed by the One who will stop at nothing to get us to look up from our iPhones for long enough to acknowledge his existence.

(As an aside, it is this very theme that U2 takes up in their song "Unknown Caller." The protagonist finds himself at the end of his rope, "lost between the midnight and the dawning, in a place of no consequence or company," when he suddenly begins to receive mysterious text messages from on high bidding him to "Hear Me, cease to speak that I may speak!" Though obviously fictional, it appears that this man's God is no less resourceful than Balaam's when it comes to getting his creatures' attention.)[3]

Social critic David Brooks has explored this theme in his book *On Paradise Drive*, the subtitle of which is "How We Live Now (And Always Have) in the Future Tense." He writes, "People have a different sense of place. They don't perceive where they live as a destination, merely as a dot on the flowing plane of multidirectional movement."[4] He continues:

---

1. Kreeft, *Three Philosophies*, 49.

2. Lewis, *Mere Christianity*, quoted in *The Quotable Lewis*, Martindale and Root, eds., 287.

3. Balaam is a character in the Old Testament book of Numbers to whom God speaks through the mouth of his donkey.

4. Brooks, *On Paradise Drive*, 4.

> [The] simple fact is that Americans move around more than any other people on earth. In any given year, 16 percent of Americans move, compared with about 4 percent of the Dutch and Germans, 8 percent of the Brits, and about 3 percent of the Thais. According to the Census Bureau's Current Population survey, only a quarter of American teenagers expect to live in their hometowns as adults, which reflects a truly radical frame of mind. Today, as always, Americans move so much and so feverishly that they change the landscape of reality more quickly than we can adjust our mental categories.[5]

Although Brooks's research indicates that such frenetic movement from place to place is something that characterizes Americans more than others, this of course does not mean that Americans feel their divine discontentment more than the rest of God's creatures. It only means that we are quicker to give expression to it, or that we do so in more extreme ways. Agrarian thinker Wendell Berry suggests that this may be due to Americans' unique history. He writes, "As a people, wherever we have been, we have never really intended to be. The continent is said to have been discovered by an Italian who was on his way to India." Of our constant movement Berry writes: "Once the unknown geography was mapped, the industrial marketplace became the new frontier, and we continued, with largely the same motives and with increasing haste and anxiety, to displace ourselves—no longer with unity of direction, like a migrant flock, but like the refugees from a broken anthill. In our time we have invaded foreign lands and the moon with the high-toned patriotism of the conquistadors, and with the same mixture of fantasy and avarice."[6]

This "displacing of ourselves," as Berry calls it, it but a symptom of a much larger existential condition, the very condition that this book wants to highlight and force us to reckon with. It is this delightful-yet-disorienting condition that St. Augustine discovered when he prayed, "God, thou hast made us for Thyself, and our hearts are restless until they find their rest in Thee." It was of the destiny of the species that the late Rich Mullins sang in "Land of My Sojourn":

> *In the place where morning gathers*
> *You can look sometimes forever till you seize*
> *What time may never know:*

---

5. Kreeft, *Three Philosophies*, 6–7.
6. Berry, *The Art of the Commonplace*, 35.

The Destiny of the Species

> *How the Lord takes by its corners this whole world*
> *And shakes us bored, and shakes us free*
> *To run wild with the hope*
> *That this dirge will not last long,*
> *But will soon drown in a song*
> *Not sung in vain.*[7]

This is precisely where we can most clearly see the distinction between man and animal. I doubt that even the most hardcore, card-carrying member of PETA would argue that ostriches are by nature divinely discontent or that bunnies pine for the afterlife. As Kreeft says, "Men live not just in the present but also in the future. We live by hope. Our hearts are a beat ahead of our feet. Half of us is already in the future; we meet ourselves coming at us from up ahead. Our lives are like an arc stretching out to us from the future into the present. Our hopes and ideals move our present lives. Animals' lives are like an arc coming to them out of their past; they are determined by their past. They are pushed; we are pulled. They are forced; we are free."[8] Thus when we insist that the distinction between man and animal is one of degree and not kind, one of quantity and not quality, we effectively rob ourselves of precisely what makes us human, namely, our frustration with things as they are. It is our recognition of injustice and evil, our wrestling with our own demons, that sick-to-our-stomach feeling we get when we watch the news that is essential to our identity as divine image-bearers. When we lose that, we become less than what we are meant to be. In short, we become like animals (only worse, for unlike them, we know better).

The Dignity of Despair

When we lose sight of the destiny of the species, we run the risk of falling into a rank kind of hedonism that is as dishonest as it is distracting. Trite platitudes about *carpe*-ing the *diem* or dying with the most toys ring hollow when we fail to affirm the central point of one of the most profound works of philosophy ever penned, the book of Ecclesiastes. There the writer says the following about all earthly toil when divorced from the ultimate, heavenly end: "Vanity of vanities, says the Preacher, vanity of vanities! All is

---

7. This song appears on Mullins's 1993 album *A Liturgy, a Legacy, and a Ragamuffin Band*.

8. Kreeft, *Three Philosophies*, 29.

vanity... I have seen everything that is done under the sun, and behold, all is vanity and a striving after wind" (Ecc. 1:1, 14). Such hypocrisy is humorously (albeit somewhat disturbingly) illustrated by an article that appeared in the satirical newspaper *The Onion* about a man who earnestly advises his friend to "seize the day" and ask his co-worker out on a date after he himself spent the previous 24 hours in a darkened room looking at Internet pornography. Needless to say, when we ceaselessly seek to distract ourselves from truths we just can't bear to confront, we aren't doing ourselves any favors. As Kreeft writes, "There are many pleasant recreations on the deck of the *Titanic*."[9]

Still, "honest hedonism is spiritually superior to dishonest self-delusion," and Jesus offered a much more stinging rebuke to the man in his parable who built bigger barns to store his possessions and then proceeded to eat, drink, and be merry than he did to the woman caught in adultery or the thief on the cross. "Infinitely superior to self-satisfied yuppiedom, Ecclesiastes has the heroism of honesty. Infinitely superior to pop psychology, it rises to the dignity of despair."[10] Contrary to the sappy and vacuous façade that often passes for sincere Christianity in the American church, the true saint's lamentation and cry of "How long?" more faithfully captures the heart of Jesus, whom one prophet described as a "man of sorrows, acquainted with grief" (Isa. 53:3). It is this "dignity of despair" that makes life livable, for without a problem there is no need for a solution, without wrong there can be no right, and without thirst there can be no satisfaction. In other words, it is not until we appreciate the severity of the question that that question becomes a quest.

"Not All Those Who Wander Are Lost"

If anyone understood the nature of a quest, it was Frodo Baggins, the unlikely hobbit-hero of J.R.R. Tolkien's epic trilogy *The Lord of the Rings*. Having discovered that he had in his possession "the One Ring" that had the power to enslave the free peoples of Middle Earth if it should fall into the wrong hands, Frodo and his trusted companions Samwise, Merry, and Pippin set out on a journey to Mount Doom in the land of Mordor, the one place where the Ring could be destroyed. Though he described his quest as

---

9. Ibid., 21.
10. Ibid.

an "exile," he embarked upon it nonetheless, for he understood the severity of the consequences that would result from his failure or success.[11]

J. Lenore Wright points out in her essay "Sam and Frodo's Excellent Adventure: Tolkien's Journey Motif," that there is a lot more to a journey than the mere movement from one geographical location to another. Some journeys, like that of St. Augustine (as outlined in his *Confessions*) are spiritual in nature, while that of the townsfolk in the film *Pleasantville* is moral and intellectual. "Although a journey involves movement—physical, spiritual, intellectual, or philosophical—there is more to a journey than reaching one's destination." Wright continues: "As Bilbo points out, 'Not all those who wander are lost' (FR, p. 278). Indeed, movement requires freedom of varying kinds, but the movement away from one's physical space and one's perspective on reality requires one to accept and act upon at least two kinds of freedom: freedom from material belongings (a freedom to uproot and wander), and freedom from conflicting duties."[12] When it comes to the theme we are considering, Bilbo's words can be echoed with even greater force than Tolkien intended. Ironically enough, in addition to saying that not all those who journey heavenward are lost, we can also insist that *it is only those who journey heavenward that are not lost*. In other words, "lostness" does not come from wandering, but from refusing to do so, and further, it is precisely by leaving that we truly become found. By digging our heels into earth and sinking our roots into this present age we demonstrate just how lost we really are, for as we saw above, man was never designed to remain tethered to the temporary, or harnessed to the here and now. In the words of Ecclesiastes, "God has put eternity into man's heart," and our job is to beware of it being eclipsed by all the things *we* put in there.

Moreover, it is through the hobbits' journey out of their comfort zone and into the unknown that they discover their true selves:

> As Frodo and his hobbit companions journey further and further from the comfortable Shire, they forge new self-identities. Though typical hobbits are passive and fearful, Sam, Merry, and Pippin face their fears and confront the horrors of war, engaging in varied forms of battle themselves. They suffer physical and psychological wounds, wounds that with each stage of healing make them stronger, braver, and more confident. As a result of the wounding and

---

11. Tolkien, *The Fellowship of the Ring*, quoted in Wright, "Sam and Frodo's Excellent Adventure: Tolkien's Journey Motif" in Bassham and Bronson (eds.) *The Lord of the Rings and Philosophy*, 195.

12. Ibid.

healing process they undergo, they unchain themselves from their natural instincts and hobbit-like desires. Only then does their physical journey become existential. Once this transformation occurs, their self-conceptions become harmonized with their duties, and they fulfill the Nietzchean charge to "become who you are."[13]

With all due respect to Friedrich, the charge to "become who you are" has roots that stretch back much further than he perhaps realized. Despite what the Enlightenment sought to teach us, there simply is no detached, objective "view from nowhere," but we all see life through lenses (whether good or bad ones). The challenge for us is to view the world and our place in it through the lens of what we know to be true of us, namely, that we have been created to enjoy heavenly, eternal rest, and that even the best that this present world can offer falls woefully short of the destiny we were made for. "Becoming what we are," therefore, is tantamount to seeing ourselves through the lens of reality as God defines it, and living accordingly.

This is why Wright insists that the hobbits forged "new self-identities" as they journeyed farther and farther from their home toward their destination. For Frodo, Sam, Merry, and Pippin, as long as the boundaries of their thought did not extend beyond the borders of the Shire, they could be content with simple pleasures like pipeweed and ale at the Green Dragon after a hard day's work in the garden. But once their vision expanded and the world got a whole lot bigger, they could no longer delude themselves into thinking that local gossip about the goings-on of the townsfolk was really the be-all/end-all of existence. No, there came a point where the hobbits simply knew too much to be charmed by life's details—they were spoiled for the Shire's spoils after beginning to see themselves in the light of a much grander and more epic struggle.

What about us? Opening ourselves up to the exciting-yet-frightening possibility that this world may not be all there is will be, on the one hand, merely admitting what we have always known to be true, but on the other hand, it will expose us to potential highs and lows that we have never imagined, let alone experienced. For example, if a person's life is lived in utter obliviousness to eternal concerns, then it is understandable that earthly ones will fill void (Will I get that promotion? Will I lose this excess weight? Will I be accepted into university?). My intention is not to belittle these questions, but to point out that there are much higher stakes to consider once we journey out of the cave (to borrow Plato's metaphor) or the Shire (to use

---

13. Ibid., 196.

The Destiny of the Species

Tolkien's). To repeat Wright's words above, "As a result of the wounding and healing process they undergo, they unchain themselves from their natural instincts and hobbit-like desires. Only then does their physical journey become existential." Now in order to apply this to the spiritual realm I must point out that it is not *we* who cure ourselves from our earthly myopia, it is not *we* who trade our old lenses for new ones, and it is not *we* who psyche ourselves up for the journey we must undertake—it is God who enables us for these things (more on this later). Still, once we are given new eyes to see, we open ourselves up to higher hopes than remodeling our kitchen, and lower laments than those which come from not getting asked to the prom. In a word, when we discover the destiny of the species, try as we might, we will become forever unable to go back to the detached, disinterested, earthbound existence that we once lived. Instead, like Frodo, we will pack our bags for pilgrimage, knowing that the trials along the way are not worthy of comparing to the glory of our final destination.

We Don't Need Another Hero

Perhaps all this talk of journeys and destiny engenders in you the question, "Who do you think I am, some warrior from Greek mythology who has so much time on my hands that I can gallivant around on my winged horse slaying dragons all day? I'm just an ordinary person with a job and family. I'm not cut out for heroics." I don't doubt that this is the case. But consider Frodo's reluctance to strike out for Mount Doom: "Of course, I have sometimes thought of going away, but I imagined that as a kind of holiday, a series of adventures like Bilbo's or better, ending in peace. But this would mean exile, a flight from danger into danger, drawing it after me. . . . But I feel very small, and very uprooted, and well—desperate. The Enemy is so strong and terrible."[14] Hardly the attitude one would equate with exploits of bravery and heroism! But this should be comforting rather than worrisome, for the journey that God calls us to is not something open only to people of valor and courage, but in fact, it's just the opposite. As Wright points out:

> Pilgrims are different from heroes in the classical sense of the term. According to both ancient mythology and modern epics, heroes are courageous, large in stature, often of divine ancestry or noble birth, sometimes magical, athletic, intelligent, adept at specific

14. Tolkien, *Fellowship of the Ring*, 69, quoted in Ibid., 200–01.

skills, and knowledgeable of the arts. . . . Classic Greek examples include Theseus, who with the help of his beloved Ariadne slays the Minotaur who guards the labyrinth in Knossos, and Odysseus, who Homer represents as the noblest and most respected hero for his courage, cunning, and eloquence.

Unlike these heroes, Sam and Frodo experience constant fear and dread; their journey is overshadowed by despair. Like all hobbits, they are small in stature, often mistaken for children. Nor are they of noble ancestry or exceptionally knowledgeable, intelligent, skilled, or athletic. Their strength lies in their devotion, determination, and single-mindedness of purpose. They are not heroes in the classical sense; rather, they exemplify the traits of modern pilgrims.[15]

Tolkien, himself a Catholic, quite possibly had the words of St. Paul in mind when developing the hobbits' characters, who wrote to the Corinthians: "For consider your calling, brothers: not many of you were wise according to worldly standards, not many were powerful, not many were of noble birth. But God chose what is foolish in the world to shame the wise; God chose what is weak in the world to shame the strong; God chose what is low and despised in the world, even things that are not, to bring to nothing things that are, so that no human being might boast in the presence of God" (I Corinthians 1:26–29). Yet even as strength and courage were given to those pilgrim-hobbits when they needed it most—Frodo appearing in Sam's eyes like "a tall stern shadow, a mighty lord who hid his brightness in grey cloud," and Sam's face becoming "stern, almost grim, as the will hardened in him, and he felt through all his limbs a thrill, as if he was turning into some creature of stone and steel that neither despair nor weariness nor endless barren miles could subdue"—so will be the case with all those who catch a glimpse of the eternal destiny that beckons those who are given eyes to see it.[16]

---

15. Ibid., 201–02.
16. Tolkien, *The Two Towers*, 383; J.R.R. Tolkien, *The Return of the King*, 225, quoted in Bassham and Bronson, *The Lord of the Rings and Philosophy*, 202.

2

The Jagged Little Red Pill

"Why," asks Alanis Morissette in her song "All I Really Want," "are you so petrified of silence?" She then challenges the listener by singing, "Here, can you handle *this*?," and what follows is about five seconds of completely dead air with neither a sound from her voice nor a note from an instrument to be heard. When the music finally resumes she asks, "Did you think about your bills, your ex, your deadlines, or when you think you're gonna die? Or did you long for the next distraction?" I think her point is that it was probably the latter.[1]

The Tyranny of the Non-Urgent

Despite the nobility and grandeur which characterize the destiny of the species, the fact is that we humans bore easily. Rather than pondering the profound we often opt for blankly staring at the superfluous, resulting in our becoming really overwhelmed with the really underwhelming. As someone who now lives in the Seattle area, I can certainly testify that there is nothing better than handheld technological gadgets to inoculate us against noticing the evidence of God's existence all around us (this is often accomplished by enabling us to tune out the world and zero in on what's really important, like which ringtones to download to my cell). Though by the time this book is published the following will already sound rather dated, as I write (as in, literally an hour ago), Apple's CEO Steve Jobs unveiled the iPad, a product so new that my computer's spell-check underlined the word in red because

---

1. "All I Really Want" is from Alanis Morissette's 1995 album *Jagged Little Pill*.

it thinks I misspelled i*Pod*, and so revolutionary that my Facebook news feed is abuzz with glee mingled with concern on the part of those whose lives have suddenly become meaningless because they don't yet have a—what's it called again?—oh yeah: an iPad.

My point is not to dismiss technology (I *am* typing on a wireless keyboard, after all) but to use it as an example to highlight the fact that we humans-made-in-God's-image often sell ourselves short, failing to find wonder in the truly wonderful. This point was humorously made by the comedian Louis CK who recently appeared on *Late Night With Conan O'Brien*. Answering Conan's question about whether people in the twenty-first century take things for granted, he replied:

> "Well, yeah. [Airline travel] is the worst one because people come back from flights and they tell you their story, and it's like a horror story, they make their flight sound like it was a cattle car in 1940s Germany. That's how bad they make it sound. They say, 'It was the worst day of my life! First of all, we didn't board for twenty minutes, and then we get on the plane and they made us sit there, on the runway, for forty minutes!' And I say, 'Oh really? And what happened next, did you *fly*, through the *air*, incredibly, like a bird? Did you partake in the miracle of human flight, you non-contributing zero? You're FLYING! It's amazing! . . . You're sitting in a chair, *in the sky.* . . .'"

He then went on to mock the man sitting next to him on the flight because he was complaining about the spotty wifi service on the plane which, by the way, he only found out existed ten minutes prior. Needless to say, when we are "consumed by the chill of solitary"[2] we not only begin to sound rather entitled, but we also forget what our hearts, deep down, have always known: that we were never designed to be satisfied with the toys of a passing age, but are meant for much more. In this chapter I will address the (natural-yet-supernatural) choice that we must make to say "No" to a culture that seeks to tether us to earth, and rather to embrace a future-focused outlook that, for all its challenges, nevertheless reflects what is real.

"The Matrix Has You"

"Propaganda," writes Thomas Merton: "*makes up our mind* for us, but in such a way that it leaves us the sense of pride and satisfaction of men

2. Ibid.

who have made up their own minds. And in the last analysis, propaganda achieves this effect *because we want it to*. This is one of the few real pleasures left to modern man: this illusion that he is thinking for himself when, in fact, someone else is doing his thinking for him."[3] Such was certainly the case for Thomas Anderson (A.K.A. "Neo"), the protagonist in the film *The Matrix*. All his life had been spent wrestling with the nagging thought that something was amiss in the world, that there was some place he was supposed to find, only he didn't know where to begin searching. To complicate matters, Neo comes to be convinced that there was this *thing* called the Matrix that represented the problem and source of his frustration, only he didn't know exactly what it was. Eventually, however, he is approached by a woman called Trinity who is a part of a subversive band of resistance fighters, and she seems to have the answers Neo is looking for (or, can lead him to the one who does):

> Trinity: "I know why you're here, Neo. I know what you've been doing . . . why you hardly sleep, why you live alone, and why night after night, you sit by your computer. You're looking for him. I know because I was once looking for the same thing. And when he found me, he told me I wasn't really looking for him. I was looking for an answer. It's the question that drives us, Neo. It's the question that brought you here. You know the question, just as I did."
>
> Neo: "What is the Matrix?"
>
> Trinity: "The answer is out there, Neo, and it's looking for you, and it will find you if you want it to."

Before long, Neo is led to a man called Morpheus (wonderfully played by Laurence Fishburne) who is the leader of the resistance. The following dialogue ensues:

> Morpheus: "I imagine that right now, you're feeling a bit like Alice. Hmm? Tumbling down the rabbit hole?"
>
> Neo: "You could say that."
>
> Morpheus: "I see it in your eyes. You have the look of a man who accepts what he sees because he is expecting to wake up. Ironically, that's not far from the truth. Do you believe in fate, Neo?"
>
> Neo: "No."
>
> Morpheus: "Why not?"

---

3. Dark, *Everyday Apocalypse*, 78, emphasis original.

Neo: "Because I don't like the idea that I'm not in control of my life."

Morpheus: "I know *exactly* what you mean. Let me tell you why you're here. You're here because you know something. What you know you can't explain, but you feel it. You've felt it your entire life, that there's something wrong with the world. You don't know what it is, but it's there, like a splinter in your mind, driving you mad. It is this feeling that has brought you to me. Do you know what I'm talking about?"

Neo: "The Matrix."

Morpheus: "Do you want to know what it is?"

Neo: "Yes."

Morpheus: "The Matrix is everywhere. It is all around us. Even now, in this very room. You can see it when you look out your window, or when you turn on your television. You can feel it when you go to work, when you go to church, when you pay your taxes. It is the world that has been pulled over your eyes to blind you from the truth."

Neo: "What truth?"

Morpheus: "That you are a slave, Neo. Like everyone else, you were born into bondage, born into a prison that you cannot smell or taste or touch. A prison for your mind. Unfortunately, no one can be told what the Matrix is. You have to see it for yourself. This is your last chance. After this, there is no turning back. You take the blue pill, the story ends, you wake up in your bed and believe whatever you want to believe. You take the red pill, you stay in Wonderland, and I show you how deep the rabbit hole goes."

Need I even say it? *Neo takes the red pill . . . .*

Seeing Through the See-Through

In order for those of us who share this frustration with earth to give expression to our longing for the transcendent over the temporal, we must also join the resistance. And on one level it shouldn't be that hard to enlist volunteers, for as I argued in the last chapter, the more we are in touch with our true humanity the more we will recognize the misplaced and displaced nature of the unmerry merry-go-round that is our lives. Whether by the market, the state, or the trends of the culture, the fact is that multitudes of

The Destiny of the Species

Americans feel as if their lives are being co-opted and commandeered by interests not their own.

This phenomenon is powerfully articulated by Naomi Klein in her book *No Logo*, which draws attention to the inroads that global corporations have made into just about every sphere of life, from public education to public space. She writes that when she began the book, " . . . my hypothesis was mostly based on a hunch. I had been doing some research on university campuses and had begun to notice that many of the students I was meeting were preoccupied with the inroads private corporations were making into their public schools. They were angry that ads were creeping into cafeterias, common rooms, even washrooms; that their schools were diving into exclusive distribution deals with soft-drink companies and computer manufacturers, and that academic studies were starting to look more and more like market research."[4] Describing her own research and accompanying journey, she continues:

> This personal quest has taken me to a London courtroom for the handing down of the verdict in the McLibel Trial; to Ken Saro-Wiwa's friends and family; to anti-sweatshop protests outside Nike Towns in New York and San Francisco; and to union meetings in the food courts of glitzy malls. It took me on the road with an "alternative" billboard salesman and on the prowl with "adbusters" out to "jam" the meaning of those billboards with their own messages. And it brought me, too, to several impromptu street parties whose organizers are determined to briefly liberate public space from its captivity by ads, cars and cops.[5]

David Dark (who in addition to being an author teaches high school English) concurs with Klein's analysis of people's attitudes toward the loss of control over their own thoughts. He says of his students that:

> They take personally the apocalyptic significance of films whose protagonists discover themselves in carefully scripted, immersive environments which create the illusion of freedom while using inhabitants to fuel their own death-dealing machinery. They know the joke's on them when a voice says, "Because we value you, our viewers/customers/clients . . . ." And the bright colors, earnest-sounding voices, and lively music only serve to remind that someone (or something) is trying to create demand and move product. . . . The sense that they've been playing roles in a vast

4. Klein, *No Logo*, xx.
5. Ibid., xxii.

formula of market research, while occasionally consoling themselves with a packaged rebellion, isn't a realization anyone can sustain for long without becoming depressed. But there is something powerfully invigorating about imagining, especially in the company of young people, what it might mean to take the red pill of reality on a regular basis or to weather the storm to the limits of one's bubble and to break on through to the other side.[6]

At our most cynical we admit that, from earth's perspective (what Ecclesiastes calls life "under the sun"), *this is what we're for*. The whole point of our existence, our taking up precious space on this planet, is to fuel the machine and to enforce the system of the *status quo*: "In *The Matrix*, we're conceived for the purpose of being plugged in. We're fuel for the prodigious machinery. The commodification knows no end."[7]

But some know better, even if they don't know how, or why. Like Neo, or like *Fight Club*'s Tyler Durden, they can stand up in protest to the dehumanizing demands of the their day:

> "I see all this potential, and I see squandering: an entire generation pumping gas, waiting tables; slaves with white collars. Advertising has us chasing cars and clothes, working jobs we hate so we can buy shit we don't need. We're the middle children of history, man. No purpose or place. We have no Great War. No Great Depression. Our Great War's a spiritual war . . . our Great Depression is our lives. We've all been raised on television to believe that one day we'd all be millionaires, and movie gods, and rock stars. But we *won't*. And we're slowly learning that fact. And we're very, *very* pissed off."

It is the ability to see through what's see-through, to penetrate the façade and steal a glimpse of the worldly wizard behind the curtain, that Dark and others refer to as "apocalyptic living." As I will argue in subsequent chapters, our native eyes and tainted perspective can only take us so far, and that ultimately God alone can provide for us the lenses through which we can truly behold the depth and degree of our servitude. For our present purposes, though, it's enough to note that, despite the world's pomp and promises, the emperor is wearing no clothes. *And many of us know it.*

---

6. Dark, *Apocalypse*, 81–82.
7. Ibid., 87.

The Destiny of the Species

Harps and Halos, or Happiness and Humanitarianism?

In our day, filled as it is with innumerable challenges that demand our immediate attention, about the worst thing one can be labeled is an "escapist." As I write, relief workers are still sifting through the rubble in Haiti to recover the bodies of those lost in the recent earthquake, while confidence here at home concerning the economy is at a serious low. With the world being filled with wars and rumors of wars and earthquakes in various places, what business do we have, it may legitimately be asked, looking ahead to heaven while earth falls apart? After all, isn't there some line about the indirect proportion of heavenly-mindedness and earthly-goodness? In a word, when one's mouth waters at the thought of "pie in the sky when you die," it doesn't exactly bode well for his hopes of earning *Time Magazine*'s "Man of the Year" award (or for that matter, a "World's Greatest Dad" coffee mug). What are we to make of this charge?

Well, it all depends. And what it depends on is something very simple: does heaven really exist, or doesn't it? If one stops to think about it, it makes perfect sense that if heaven is ultimate and earth is only penultimate, then settling for the latter is not only foolish, but indeed masochistic. Why would anyone take the temporal instead of the eternal, or prefer the provisional over the permanent?

But before we sheepishly look down at our feet and cop to the charge of escapism, we need to make a few qualifications. First, if, as I said, heaven actually exists, then my wanting to go there is only as escapist as is the desire of a fetus to be born. Heaven is to earth what the outside world is to the womb, so if there is such a thing as birth, it follows that the womb is temporary, and if there is such a thing as the new birth, then earth must be temporary as well (more on the new birth later). As Peter Kreeft says, "'There is a tunnel under this prison' may be an escapist idea, *but it may also be true.*"[8] In other words, whether or not a hope is escapist is incidental to whether that hope is grounded in fact. If it is factual, then its being escapist is beside the point. Consider Kreeft's parable:

> There was a rumor among the caterpillars that they were destined to become butterflies. Some caterpillars believed it; others disbelieved; and still others doubted. Now what would be the reasonable attitude of each of the three groups of caterpillars toward this rumor? Which could reasonably call it escapist? Would not even

8. Kreeft, *Heaven*, 164, emphasis added.

the uncertain want to explore it further? For if it is true ... it is not escapism. The charge of escapism therefore logically boils down to the charge of falsehood; only those who are certain the rumor is false can reasonably call it escapist. Otherworldliness is escapism only if there is no other world. If there is, it is worldliness that is escapism.[9]

"*Worldliness* is escapism"—what an absolutely profound point! To put it differently, the only way the escapist label will stick is if the one applying it knows, beyond a shadow of doubt, that heaven doesn't exist. But this kind of certainty is impossible, which reduces the charge of escapism to mere wishful thinking on the part of the one making it. But if the person who dismisses the desire for heaven has nothing to base his suspicions on beyond what he merely wishes to be true (or not to be true, in this case), then who is the real escapist here? Is it possible that the skeptic's true motives are being revealed, and what lurks behind his confidence and posturing is the desire not to escape *to* heaven, but to escape *from* it? After all, it's easier to avoid God than to embrace Him, just as it was easier for the prodigal son to leave home than it was for him to return.

And secondly, what are we to make of the claim that being too heavenly-minded means that we will be of no earthly good? If we spend too much time thinking about harps and halos, will we lose all interest in earthly happiness and humanitarianism? Following Kreeft, let's answer the question with a question: Who is more likely to quit smoking during pregnancy, the mother who plans for an abortion or the one who plans to give birth? The answer should be obvious. Roads that actually lead somewhere are usually better maintained than dead-end ones, and likewise, when our earthly sojourn is seen as just that—a sojourn on the way to our heavenly home—then it is reasonable to assume that this pilgrimage will be taken with great seriousness and care. If death, as all the world's major religions teach, is not the end of the road, but actually ushers us into the presence of the God who gave us life and demands an account of how we lived it, then is it not to be expected that the pilgrim with an eye on his destination will live more purposefully than will the tourist, the goal of whose trip is to get as much bang as possible for his buck?[10]

---

9. Ibid., 168.
10. See http://www.peterkreeft.com/topics/heaven.htm.

The Destiny of the Species

"Follow the White Rabbit"

Returning to *The Matrix*, when Neo first makes contact with the resistance, the cryptic instruction he is given is to "Follow the White Rabbit," and it is by deciphering this clue that he is eventually liberated from the Lie and given eyes to see. In fact, when he is finally awoken from his slumber and his body is unplugged from the Matrix, he asks Morpheus, "Why do my eyes hurt?" and receives the curt reply, "Because you've never used them before."

In *Everyday Apocalypse*, Dark quotes at length from Claude Tresmontant's *Christian Metaphysics*, in which he writes: "The child is not born in Paradise. It is born in a criminal humanity. In order to have access to justice, to sanctity, the child, as it grows up, will have to make a personal act of judgment, of refusal, of choice. It will have to make a personal act of opposition to the values of its tribe, its nation, its caste, its class, its race.... Holiness begins with a breach. Nothing can dispense the child from this personal act of breaking with 'the world.'"[11] Dark then comments: "It's the absence of such carefully wrought, imaginative explanations in the popular and most-widely aired conceptions of Christianity (the 'broadcast' versions) that makes *The Matrix* such a revolutionary film. It gives us a sense of sin and salvation which might actually have some bearing on the way we think and live within the world."[12]

In chapter 5 I will delve more deeply into the issue of what earthly ties hinder us from embracing our God-given identity and pursuing the destiny of the species, but for our purposes here it is sufficient to say that we, like Neo (and Alice before him), must follow the white rabbit and be willing to tumble down that hole, wherever it may lead us. Any institution or worldview whose aim is to lull us to sleep and make us forget about all these transcendental questions must be seen for what it is: "a tacit (and sometimes not so tacit) sponsor of the powers that be, *not* the resistance force that might overcome them through radical, alternative, apocalyptic living."[13] Such counter-insurgency may be tactically employed by the media, the market, or the megachurch (are they really all that different?), but regardless of its source, it must be rejected as the anesthetizing and inoculating—not to mention dehumanizing—poison that it is. As C.S. Lewis put

---

11. Quoted in Dark, *Apocalypse*, 90.
12. Ibid.
13. Ibid., 90–91.

it, "If we insist on keeping Hell (or even earth) we shall not see Heaven. If we accept Heaven we shall not be able to retain even the smallest souvenir of Hell."[14]

On Maniacs and Mystics

"Hang on a minute," you may be thinking. "Isn't all this talk of red pills and rabbit holes just a tad, I don't know, *insane*? Aren't you making too much out of these fictional fairy tales? Why shouldn't I stick to what I can understand, like logic, or what I can see, like the world around me?" These are sensible objections, but if you think about it, they are completely wrongheaded. As always, G.K. Chesterton is helpful here: "Imagination does not breed insanity. Exactly what does breed insanity is reason. Poets do not go mad; but chess-players do. . . . The poet only desires exaltation and expansion, a world to stretch himself in. The poet only asks to get his head into the heavens. It is the logician who seeks to get the heavens into his head. And it is his head that splits."[15] In other words, what constitutes insanity is not the abandonment of reason (as if I am suggesting any such thing), but the abandonment of everything else.

Why does reason alone, when devoid of the mysterious and otherworldly, breed insanity? Why does atheism drive us much more crazy than theism ever could? The answer is (and the feeling you're about to experience is called irony) that a materialist, atheistic worldview is far more restricting than one that affirms the existence of God, of the afterlife, and—if Chesterton has anything to say about it—of fairies. "Even if I believe in immortality," he writes, "I need not think about it. But if I disbelieve in immortality I must not think about it. In the first case the road is open and I can go as far as I like; in the second the road is shut."[16] He continues: "Mysticism keeps men sane. As long as you have mystery you have health; when you destroy mystery you create morbidity. The ordinary man has always been sane because the ordinary man has always been a mystic. He has permitted the twilight. He has always had one foot in the earth and the other in fairyland. He has always left himself free to doubt his gods; but (unlike the agnostic of today) free also to believe in them."[17]

---

14. Lewis, *The Great Divorce*, quoted in *The Quotable Lewis*, 282.
15. Chesterton, *Orthodoxy*, 14, 15.
16. Ibid., 30.
17. Ibid., 31.

The Destiny of the Species

Chesterton is making a very important point here that we would do well not to miss. The charge, so common in our day, that faith, mystery, or otherworldliness are somehow confining or restrictive is patently false. The open-minded theist may, if he pleases, quietly thank God for the birth of his first child, but the atheist may do no such thing since he lives in a strictly physical universe closed off to any and all spiritual intrusion. To quote Adam Sandler's character from his film *The Wedding Singer*, "We're living in a material world and I am a material girl. Or *boy*." As Chesterton insists, when we reduce all reality to the tyranny of the empirical (what we can see, hear, or touch), we succeed in muddying the waters despite our attempts to clarify them. The "morbid logician" tries to make everything clear but ends up making *everything* a mystery. The mystic, on the other hand, by insisting that *one thing* is mysterious, makes everything else lucid. In other words, "The whole secret of mysticism is this: that man can understand everything by the help of what he does not understand."[18] And that one thing, of course, is God.

These two ways of looking at the world, Chesterton says, can be summarized by two familiar symbols: the circle and the cross. The circle has always been understood to symbolize strict reason and the madness that accompanies it, while the cross is the icon of mystery and of health. And if you think about it, it makes perfect sense. The former is indeed perfect in its nature, but it is also fixed in its size and can never expand without doing damage to itself (next time you're chewing gum, try blowing a bubble the size of Seattle if you don't believe me). A cross, on the other hand, is not nearly as neat and tidy as a circle—it has at its very heart a paradox, the collision of two perpendicular lines. But those lines, Chesterton reminds us, can extend their four arms forever without altering the cross's shape: "Because it has a paradox at its centre it can grow without changing. The circle returns upon itself and is bound. The cross opens its arms to the four winds; it is the signpost for free travelers."[19]

Corresponding to the symbols of the circle and the cross are the moon on the one hand and the sun on the other. The sun, like God himself, is the one thing we cannot look at, but in the light of which we can look at everything else. But detached and clinical intellectualism, quips Chesterton, is "all moonshine," for "it is light without heat, and it is secondary light, reflected from a dead world." He continues: "But that transcendentalism by

18. Ibid., 32.
19. Ibid., 33.

which all men live has primarily much the position of the sun in the sky. We are conscious of it as a kind of splendid confusion; it is something both shining and shapeless, at once a blaze and a blur. But the circle of the moon is as clear and unmistakable, as recurrent and inevitable, as the circle of Euclid on a blackboard. For the moon is utterly reasonable; and the moon is the mother of lunatics and has given to them all her name."[20] After all, the term "lunatic" has as its root the Latin word *luna*, which, of course, means "moon."

The objection that man's need to pursue the destiny of the species reflects a kind of wacky mysticism, therefore, falls flat. In fact, I would go so far as to insist upon the very opposite, namely, that until man embraces his identity as one created for everlasting glory, he will never be truly sane. Being willing to take the red pill, jagged though it may be, is precisely what will unlock the door into a strange new world that, though it will never be fully understood, will nonetheless provide the light by which we may understand everything else.

---

20. Ibid., 33–34.

3

Which Came Last, the Chicken or the Egg?

WE HAVE SEEN THUS far that all people, whether we realize it or not, are made with a built-in desire for eternity. This longing for the future, as I explained in the previous chapter, is not just some disposition to be entertained, but it involves a choice whether to embrace our destiny or to reject it.

As I hinted at earlier, merely recognizing that something is amiss with life as we know it is not enough to bring us to the place where we will actually choose the apocalyptic, future-focused road. Bad news alone won't make us take the red pill. If we desire to avoid the charge of escapism, then allowing ourselves to long for heaven must be more than a mere coping device designed to take our minds off how much we lament our earthly lot. No, a legitimate otherworldliness must arise not only from an appreciation of the badness of this age (or for that matter, the goodness of the next), but from the fact that eternal blessedness is what we are uniquely designed *for*. In other words, heaven is meant to be just as attractive a goal for the one who enjoys his present life as it is for the one who wants to escape it. In this chapter I will further explore the theme of man's eternal destiny, focusing especially on the fact that our future is the best vantage point from which to view the present.

Which Came Last, the Chicken or the Egg?

Contrary to what one might think after perusing the "Christian Fiction" section of the local Barnes and Noble, it is not just evangelicals or fundamentalists who are preoccupied with better days ahead. Theologians and sociologists alike have often pondered the influence that man's end has upon his life in the here and now, the sway that tomorrow holds over today. As I stated earlier, secular cultural commentator David Brooks insists that man has always lived in the future tense, and a mere flip through the pages of progressive and left-wing writers such as Naomi Klein, Matt Taibbi, and David Sirota will be more than enough to convince us that it is not just religious people who bet their bottom dollar that the sun'll come out tomorrow. In a word, looking ahead is what makes us human, and future-focused man shall not live by *Left Behind* novels alone.

Unlike many attempts to diagnose man's present condition and then go on to prescribe a cure, G.K. Chesterton has provocatively suggested that this approach may be wrong-headed. Man's "dignity" as a creature made in God's image demands the opposite approach: "The first great blunder of sociology . . . is stating the disease before we find the cure. But it is the whole definition and dignity of man that in social matters we must actually find the cure before we find the disease."[1] Chesterton's point is that man can only be understood from the vantage point of the future, after running on ahead of himself, as it were, and then looking back.

The way Chesterton illustrates his point is by considering anew the famous quandary, "Which came first, the chicken or the egg?" As anyone who has considered the dilemma knows, if we say that the chicken came first we cannot answer where it came from, and if we say that the egg came first then we are faced with the question of what laid it. Chesterton's solution is to reword the problem altogether. The bigger issue, he says, is not which came first, but which comes *last*: "Leaving the complications of the human breakfast-table out of account, in an elemental sense, the egg only exists to produce the chicken. But the chicken does not exist only in order to produce another egg. He may also exist to amuse himself, to praise God, and even to suggest ideas to a French dramatist. Being a conscious life, he is, or may be, valuable in himself."[2] In other words, regardless of what may come at the beginning of the pattern, it is certain what comes at the end of it, and that is a chicken. While chickens indeed lay eggs as one of their many functions, eggs only do one thing, and that is produce chickens. "One is a means," he says, "and the other an end."

What is Chesterton's point? Well, when we are seeking to understand the human condition we must first consider what lies at the end of the road

1. Chesterton, *What's Wrong with the World*, 3.
2. Ibid., 6.

rather than merely considering what was there at the beginning of it. "The only way to discuss the social evil is to get at once to the social ideal. . . . I have called this book *What's Wrong with the World?*, and the upshot of the title can be easily and clearly stated. What is wrong is that we do not ask what is right."[3] As C.S. Lewis used to say, before we can recognize a crooked line as crooked, we must first have some idea of what a straight one would look like.

Chesterton's point, then, is that man's future says more about his present than his past ever could. In order to understand why we are here, therefore, we need to think in more ultimate and (to use Chesterton's words) idealistic terms than we are often accustomed to doing. When we think solely in terms of the pressing and immediate—which is so easy to do in our culture—we can easily come to the unwitting conclusion that we have no true end at all, that we are but ghosts in the machine, spirits in a material world. But are we really only coppertops to power the Matrix? Is satisfying the demands of the market all we're here for? Should our motto really be "I Consume, Therefore I Am"?

Absolutely not. When we accept Chesterton's dare to think idealistically, we will finally begin to realize that we were made with an ideal, a goal, in mind that we either are, or are not, living up to. Chickens are not just egg-laying machines, and likewise, you are not a mere worker or consumer—you are meant for much more than that.

By saying that we need to be more idealistic, Chesterton means that we must "consider everything in its practical essence" or what it is ideally designed for. He points out that "Idealism only means that we should consider a poker in reference to poking before we discuss its suitability for wife-beating." He continues:

> But I know that this primary pursuit of the theory (which is but pursuit of the aim) exposes one to the cheap charge of fiddling while Rome is burning. . . . There has arisen in our time a most singular fancy: the fancy that when things go very wrong we need a practical man. It would be far truer to say, that when things go very wrong we need an unpractical man. Certainly, at least, we need a theorist. A practical man means a man accustomed to mere daily practice, to the way things commonly work. When things will not work, you must have the thinker, the man who has some doctrine about why they work at all. It is wrong to fiddle while

---

3. Ibid., 5.

> Rome is burning; but it is quite right to study the theory of hydraulics while Rome is burning.[4]

You and I, therefore, will never truly understand who we are unless we are willing to "get ahead of ourselves" in a very real sense. It is only from up ahead looking back, and never from behind looking forward, that we can ever hope to gain any real perspective on who we are, and what we're for.

> In this sense, apocalyptic is the place where the future pushes into the present. It's the breaking in of another dimension, a new wine for which our old wineskins are unprepared. That which apocalyptic proclaims cannot be fit into existing ways of thinking. . . . Whether it's trees clapping their hands, stars falling from the sky, bloody red moons, or crystal seas, it's as if the new world on its way requires constant rearticulation to best bear witness of its freshness and new-every-morningness, perpetually straining forward to what lies ahead. [T]he groaning universe [is] anticipating a new day. This is the business of apocalyptic.[5]

Itching Beneath the Mask

It is precisely here that the real difficulty (at which I hinted in the last chapter) becomes increasingly overt. If "our Great War is a spiritual war" as Tyler Durden says, then we should expect to be resisted when we begin to question the mold into which the culture desires to squeeze us. The way the New Testament describes the forces of this present world is by categorizing all of earth's temptations in terms of its passions, possessions, and position (I John 2:16), and the more we seek to resist such earth-bound futility (as these pursuits surely are when divorced from eternity), the more we will be greeted with blank stares at best, and blatant scorn at worst.

Thomas Merton suggests that all people possess a true self (which is a mystery largely hidden) and a false self (the identity we try to cultivate in order to function in society). The root of all sin—what the culture euphemizes as "disorder"—is in our assuming that the false self is the true one. Since we are prone to believe the lie that this world is all there is (despite the internal scream of "No!" that we considered in chapter 1), we do everything we can to prop up the façade and seek fuel for the illusion. Merton writes:

4. Ibid., 7.
5. Dark, *Apocalypse*, 12–13.

The Destiny of the Species

> All sin starts from the assumption that my false self, the self that exists only in my own egocentric desires, is the fundamental reality to which everything else is ordered. Thus I use up my life in the desire for pleasures and the thirst for experience, for power, honor, knowledge, and love to clothe this false self and construct its nothingness into something objectively real. And I wind experiences around myself and cover myself with pleasures and glory like bandages in order to make myself perceptible to myself and to the world, as if I were an invisible body that could become visible only when something visible covered its surface.[6]

The image Merton uses is indeed vivid and evocative: Until a person discovers the destiny of the species he thinks of himself as The Invisible Man who, in order to be seen by himself and others, must desperately hunt for whatever worldly experiences and pleasures he can find in order to wrap them around himself so that others don't bump into him on the sidewalk. Perhaps even more vivid is the picture Merton paints of man according to which, by his "spiritual double-vision" that deludes him into thinking like the world wants him to, man actually betrays God's truth and loses the integrity of his own soul, thus splitting himself in two. And to make matters worse, we soon become like two shadows rather than one person, eventually forgetting which one of us is real. Thus the greater the degree to which man avoids grappling with his own divinely-given destiny, the more hopeless will become his thoughts, and the more frenetic will become his activity as he seeks to distract himself from his own spiritual schizophrenia. "He becomes his own slave driver," Merton says. "A shadow whipping a shadow to death."[7]

After a lifetime of such self-delusion and mask-wearing, we begin to think that the mask is our true face. Merton insists that the real aim of society is seen in this very pursuit. He writes: "This seems to be the collective endeavor of society: the more busily men dedicate themselves to it, the more certainly it becomes a collective illusion, until in the end we have the enormous, obsessive, uncontrollable dynamic of fabrications designed to protect mere fictitious identities—'selves,' that is to say, regarded as objects. Selves that can stand back and see themselves having fun (an illusion which reassures them that they are real)."[8] Such a pitiful pretense for living has

---

6. Merton, *Seeds*, 3.
7. Ibid., 4, 5.
8. Ibid., 3.

been captured by the bumper sticker that every third BMW displayed during the decadent 1980s: "He Who Dies with the Most Toys Wins."

Yet once we reckon with what we already know deep down, we will realize that such rationalizations, however humorously intended, accomplish little by way of soothing the true self. As long as we segregate our God-given desire for heaven from our earthly desire for fulfillment in the here and now we will allow ourselves to be continually pushed deeper and deeper into whatever pursuits the powers that be deem fitting and fun for us to engage in. The world (which Merton refers to as "the collectivity") will indeed promise to satisfy our needs, as long as we behave and obey its rules. The more we submit to it, the more power it usurps over our lives, increasing our needs and tightening its demand for conformity on our part (a kind of thank-offering for its meeting the so-called needs it created in the first place).

> Thus you can become all the more committed to the collective illusion in proportion to becoming more hopelessly mortgaged to collective power. How does this work? The collectivity informs and shapes your will to happiness ("have fun") by presenting you with irresistible images of yourself as you would like to be: having *fun that is so perfectly credible that it allows no interference of conscious doubt.* In theory such a good time can be so convincing that you are no longer aware of even a remote possibility that it might change into something less satisfying. In practice, expensive fun always admits of a doubt, which blossoms out into another full-blown need, which then calls for a still more credible and more costly refinement of satisfaction, which again fails you. The end of the cycle is despair.[9]

The irony in all of this is that in such a vicious cycle, the only thing that can substitute for happiness is the pursuit of happiness, and Desire, ever the demanding mistress, becomes an end in itself:

> *She's the dollars, she's my protection;*
> *She's the promise in the year of election;*
> *Oh, sister, I can't let you go,*
> *You're like a preacher stealing hearts*
> *At a travelling show.*[10]

---

9. Ibid., 5–6, emphasis original.
10. This quote is from the song "Desire" from U2's 1988 album *Rattle and Hum*.

The Destiny of the Species

In a word, we're all mask-wearers. Here's the thing about masks, though: you can only wear them for so long before they start to itch. Just ask any parent who has taken her children trick-or-treating: before you have successfully rung three doorbells the mask will be torn from the child's face and you will end up carrying it for the duration of the night. Now when it comes to the sophisticated, adult kind of mask-wearing, one of three avenues is usually pursued. Either we become accustomed to our mask, or we do not. If we do not, then either we seek its removal altogether (which may be the first step towards freedom), or more commonly, we attempt to trade it in for the one that someone else has on.

Those who choose door #1 are those whom the Bible describes as being blinded in eye and hardened in heart (John 12:40), who walk "in the futility of their minds; they are darkened in their understanding, alienated from the life of God because of the ignorance that is in them. . . . They have become callous and have given themselves up to sensuality, greedy to practice every kind of impurity" (Eph. 4:17–19). Of course, we cannot peer into other people's hearts (it's challenging enough to discern the complexities of our own), but we have all known people who, as far as we can tell, give absolutely no evidence whatsoever of being self-reflective enough to question whether there really is any higher calling than having the perfect job or the perfect body (and hopefully both). But rest assured, you who have made it this far into this book cannot possibly fall into category #1!

The second group of people are those whose masks have begun to itch with discomfort, and who long for its removal. In my own life, it was not until my freshman year of high school that it started to become increasingly (and painfully) obvious to me that just about everyone I knew—many since elementary school—was desperately trying to fulfill some role that they either chose for themselves, or that was chosen for them by someone else. Thinking back on it, I am reminded of the five students in the quintessential '80s teen film *The Breakfast Club* who, for various reasons, were sentenced to spend an entire Saturday in detention for their misdeeds at school. Although they were each told by the teacher assigned to supervise them to write a thousand-word essay explaining "who you think you are," the detainees (whose nine hours of seclusion eventually enabled them to shed their masks and truly see one another for the first time) decided to ignore the assignment, and instead left for him a letter which simply read: "Dear Mr. Vernon, We accept the fact that we had to sacrifice a whole Saturday in detention for whatever it was we did wrong, but we think you're crazy to make us write an essay telling you who we think we are. What do you care? You see us as you want to see us. In the simplest terms, and most convenient definitions, you see us as a brain, an athlete, a basket case, a princess, and a criminal. Does that answer your question? Sincerely yours, The Breakfast Club."

(What is especially interesting to note for our purposes here is the oft-overlooked fact that this letter is read both at the very beginning and the very end of the film, and the two versions are slightly different. In the initial reading [reflected above], the identities of the students are presented through the lens of Mr. Vernon's simplistic perception of them. But after the day has ended and the masks have been painfully torn off, the letter reflects the newly-discovered fact that the students have much more in common than the strict rules of high school social hierarchy ever allowed them to recognize. "What we found out," the final version of the letter says, "is that *each one of us* is a brain, and an athlete, a basket case, a princess, and a criminal." In other words, each student took a piece of the others with them and would carry it around forever, despite the fact that some admitted that they would not acknowledge the others when Monday rolled around.)

The third category of mask-wearers is the most dangerous of all, and consists of those whose masks have begun to itch, but who have wrongly diagnosed their malady, concluding that the real problem is the type of mask they're wearing, not the fact that they're wearing one in the first place. This is the case with those who are aware that there is such a thing as the destiny of the species (though like Neo, they may not know what exactly it is), but who nevertheless insist on fooling themselves into thinking that what really matters is the façade. This person is similar to the one considered in option 1: he also opts for the illusion over what is real. Only mask-wearer #3 is far worse, for his situation is not a result of mere ignorance, but is one of his own choosing.

Not surprisingly, there is a character in *The Matrix* who plays this very role. His name is Cipher and, in true Judas-like fashion, he agrees to betray Morpheus, Neo, and the rest of the resistance, only his price is not thirty pieces of silver, but something far more pathetic. In return for his betrayal, all Cipher wants is to be re-inserted into the Matrix, to wake up in the morning and completely forget everything he currently knows. He doesn't want to remember that the world he is experiencing is a lie, that he is a slave, that he is merely doing the bidding of the powers that be like a marionette blissfully unconcerned with who is pulling its strings.

The Destiny of the Species

Early on in the film, Cipher begins to show signs of weakening, saying, "I'm tired, Trinity. Tired of this war, tired of fighting." In the scene in which Cipher finally commits his betrayal, we see him sitting in a fancy restaurant with Agent Smith, the man tasked with quashing the resistance. Cipher cuts a piece of steak and holds up his fork and says, "You know, I know this steak doesn't exist. I know that when I put it in my mouth, the Matrix is telling my brain that it is juicy and delicious. After nine years, you know what I realize? [Takes a bite] . . . *Ignorance is bliss*." The only specific request that Cipher has for his new life of blissful ignorance in the Matrix is as follows: "I want to be rich. You know, someone important, *like an actor*." The line is indeed humorous, at least until we realize how accurately it reflects the priorities of our celebrity-obsessed culture.

Wherever we happen to fall—whether we've never been self-reflective enough to notice our own mask, whether we have noticed it and longed for its removal, or whether we simply wish to be lulled back to sleep so we can forget about the whole thing—what we must grapple with is the simple fact that these questions cannot be dismissed as interesting fodder for discussion (the way one might reflect for three or four minutes upon the insights of Dr. Phil). These truths we are considering concern the very core of our being, the ignoring of which can only lead to alienation, not to mention peril.

> Alienation begins when culture divides me against myself, puts a mask on me, gives me a role I may or may not want to play. Alienation is complete when I become completely identified with my mask, totally satisfied with my role, and convince myself that any other identity or role is inconceivable. The man who sweats under his mask, whose role makes him itch with discomfort, who hates the division in himself, is already beginning to be free. But God help him if all he wants is the mask the other man is wearing, just because the other one does not seem to be sweating or itching. Maybe he is no longer human enough to itch (or else he pays a psychiatrist to scratch him).[11]

Needless to say, although a mask may be a convenient shield to hide behind as we seek to portray a false view of ourselves to the world, the fact is that it either suffocates those who are aware of it, or lulls to sleep those who aren't (and either way, the road is vain and its end is death).

Plus, God sees right through it anyway . . . .

---

11. Merton, *Seeds*, 9–10.

Bananas and BlackBerrys

Who is it that really defines us? Who provides the narrative that shapes our true identity? When all is said and done, who gets to tell us who we are?

Make no mistake, if we deny the destiny of the species as God defines it, there is no lack of pretenders who will rush at the chance to fill the void. Among them are those who insist that things like goodness and truth are mere societal conventions invented by people who are little more than highly-evolved monkeys who climbed down from their trees, put on suits, and went to work. But is that all we are, animals who merely exchanged their bananas for BlackBerrys?

As I hope to demonstrate below, humanity enjoys much greater nobility than that. Chesterton, upon his discovery of the Christian faith and its insistence that man in his dignified-though-fallen condition was to display a kind of proud humility, said:

> Man was to be haughtier than he had ever been before; in another way he was to be humbler than he had ever been before. In so far as I am Man I am the chief of creatures. In so far as I am *a* man I am the chief of sinners. All humility that had meant pessimism, that had meant man taking a vague or mean view of his whole destiny—all that was to go. We were to hear no more the wail of Ecclesiastes that humanity had no pre-eminence over the brute, or the awful cry of Homer that man was only the saddest of all the beasts of the field. Man was a statue of God walking about the garden. Man had pre-eminence over all the brutes; man was only sad because he was not a beast, but a broken god.[12]

As much as I love Chesterton—especially his ability to portray paradox—I must admit that I prefer Brennan Manning's description: "When I get honest, I admit that I am a bundle of paradoxes. . . . Aristotle said I am a rational animal; I say I am an angel with an incredible capacity for beer."[13]

The point here is simply that we mustn't lose sight of our divinely-ordained destiny amid the dust and dirt and distraction of this passing age. Yes, the chicken is indeed produced by the egg, and, likewise, we are the product of our ancestry in some respect. But all of that pales in light of the deeper question of what the chicken is *for*. And likewise with us. Just as the chicken wasn't made to be a mere egg-layer, so you were not designed

---

12. Chesterton, *Orthodoxy*, 138–39, emphasis original.
13. Manning, *The Ragamuffin Gospel*, 22.

The Destiny of the Species

to dutifully play the role and follow the script that those in power are so willing to dole out to their subjects. There is one Playwright and Casting Director, who alone reserves the right to tell you who you are and where you fit into the story he is telling. And in this divine tale, saying that "They lived happily ever after" is a horrendous understatement.

4

The Unmerry Merry-Go-Round

WHENEVER SOMEONE PICKS UP a Bible for the first time and begins to look for a good place to begin reading, the chances are pretty slim that he or she would choose the book of Ecclesiastes as a wise place to start. In the same way that one's introduction to the medium of film is not likely to be *Hotel Rwanda*, or that *Zooropa* would be an odd choice to introduce one to the music of U2, so with this most unique of all biblical books. Ecclesiastes is as dark as it gets, and unless one wants to close the Bible and hurl himself in front of an oncoming bus, conventional wisdom would dictate that he begin with something a bit more, I don't know, cheery (like *The Joshua Tree*, or Psalm 23).

But conventional wisdom was made to be questioned. Sometimes light is the backdrop for darkness, but in other instances it is darkness that is the context for light. In the case of Ecclesiastes, it can be said that it is "the contrast, the alternative, to the rest of the Bible, the question to which the rest of the Bible is the answer. There is nothing more meaningless than an answer without its question. That is why we need Ecclesiastes."[1] Peter Kreeft speaks of Ecclesiastes as being like a photograph (which literally means "light-writing"), for its method is one of simple observation of life in the light provided "under the sun," which in Ecclesiastes is shorthand for earthly, temporal life divorced from eternal considerations. "That is the method of Ecclesiastes: simple observation. Unlike all the other books in the Bible, it has no faith flashbulb attached to its camera to reveal the inner depths or hidden meanings of life. It uses only the available light 'under the

---

1. Kreeft, *Three Philosophies*, 19.

sun': sense observation and human reason. The surface of life appears in this book with total clarity, brutal honesty, and spiritual poverty. Ecclesiastes is the truest picture of the surface that has ever been written."[2] In this chapter I will direct our thoughts not to the depths, but to the shallows, not to the profundity, but to the surface. Our purpose will be to examine life in its most natural and non-flattering light in order to discover just how futile it all can be when divorced from the world to come.

"Sliding Down the Surface of Things"[3]

"Black grace"—this was Fulton Sheen's description of divine revelation by means of darkness rather than by means of light. Ecclesiastes plays this role, for it provides the dark backdrop against which the rest of Scripture can be read and appreciated: "It is divine revelation precisely in being the absence of divine revelation. It is like the silhouette of the rest of the Bible. . . . In this book God reveals to us exactly what life is like when God does not reveal to us what life is like. Ecclesiastes frames the Bible as death frames life."[4] The reason why Ecclesiastes is important for postmodern readers today is the same reason why it was important for moderns and premoderns in times past: It has a unique way of succinctly distilling the essence of earthly life and showing it for the farce that it is. In this way, Ecclesiastes is not far from contemporary satire, for it dares to portray earthly activity and toil in a way that is stripped of all pretense to ultimate meaning or delusions of grandeur.

By way of illustration, consider a television program like NBC's *The Office*. The show is shot as a "mockumentary," the most distinctive feature of which is the fact that the characters are completely aware of the camera that's filming them, and acknowledge it regularly (as if they were in a reality TV program). Now if you were to visit the New York corporate offices of *The Office*'s fictional Dunder Mifflin Paper Company and talk to CEO David Wallace, you would most likely hear glowing tales about how important the work they are doing is, and what wonderful opportunities lie in store for all who are privileged enough to be employed by his company. But when you watch the program, which centers around the goings-on in the

---

2. Ibid.

3. This is a line from U2's song "Even Better Than the Real Thing" from their 1991 album *Achtung Baby*.

4. Kreeft, *Three Philosophies*, 23.

office of Dunder Mifflin's branch in Scranton, PA—well, you get a different story altogether: the work is humorously mundane, and the only person who takes very seriously what he does is Dwight, whose earnestness and zeal are meant to be reasons for the viewing audience to pity him (the early episodes of the show often revolved around his haggling with his boss over whether his title can be changed to "Assistant Regional Manager" rather than "Assistant *to the* Regional Manager").

Of course, I am not intending to devalue work in and of itself, for it is obviously important and necessary. But when work becomes an end rather than a means to an end, or, when we live to work rather than work to live, then the specter of Ecclesiastes is lurking not too far off.

The Five Vanities

Kreeft boils down Ecclesiastes' beef with earth to five essential "vanities," or features of life under the sun that make it futile when disconnected from anything otherworldly: "1. The sameness and indifference of all things; 2. Death as the certain and final end of life; 3. Time as a cycle of endless repetition; 4. Evil as the perennial and unsolvable problem; and 5. God as an unknowable mystery."[5] He describes them as cancers, each of which is deadly on its own. But earthly life is infected with all five.

Concerning the sameness and indifference of the universe, Kreeft insists that we humans make value judgments all the time, rightly preferring truth to falsehood, good to evil, Lakers to Celtics, *et cetera* (that last example is mine, and one with which I highly doubt the esteemed Boston College professor would concur). The universe, on the other hand, seems to display very little by way of such value judgments, allowing bad things to happen to good people (and the other way around): "Again I saw that under the sun the race is not to the swift, nor the battle to the strong, nor bread to the wise, nor riches to the intelligent, nor favor to those with knowledge, but time and chance happen to them all" (Ecc. 9:11). When considered solely in the light of earth, the universe seems to yawn and file its nails in utter disinterest when we are experiencing our highest highs or our lowest lows, as if to shrug with detachment and pronounce a deafening "So what?" over all that befalls us, good, bad, or ugly.

The second of the five vanities is death (I will devote an entire chapter to death and evil later in this book, giving what I trust is a less grim account

5. Ibid., 45–51.

of it than I will offer here). "As soon as we are born," Kreeft says, "we begin to die. We are all equally bankrupt, some of us have not yet declared: the small and arrogant oligarchy of the living, surrounded by the far more populous democracy of the dead."[6] Ecclesiastes says, "For what happens to the children of man and what happens to the beasts is the same; as one dies, so dies the other. They all have the same breath, and man has no advantage over the beasts, for all is vanity. All go to one place. All are from the dust, and to dust all return" (3:19–20). As one songwriter put it:

> *Death is everywhere,*
> *There are flies on the windscreen, for a start;*
> *Reminding us:*
> *We could be torn apart*
> *Tonight.*[7]

The third example of vanity, according to Kreeft, is time. This point was humorously made by the satirical newspaper *The Onion* under the headline, "Everything Taking Too Long." The article goes on:

> WASHINGTON—An overwhelming sense of restlessness and impatience engulfed the U.S. this week when citizens determined that everything—the morning commute, phone conversations, getting a table at Chili's, making coffee, commercial breaks, everything—was taking entirely too long.
> "This is ridiculous," said Boston resident Joe Sosnoff, waiting for a subway train running behind schedule. "I don't have time for this. I seriously do not have time for this."
> A Department of the Interior report released Wednesday stated that there are 6 trillion such instances that could not possibly go any slower if they tried, some of which include budget meetings, shaving, the act of waiting, upward mobility, microwaving that lasagna, settling down and starting a family, walking from one place to another, searching for a misplaced item, returning to the place you initially walked from, air travel, 2009, and the time it takes for a sent e-mail to arrive in someone's inbox.

This may be a difficult one for many Americans to grasp, especially since we have collectively bought into the myth of progress that has so characterized our culture and national identity. While it used to be the case that, as the saying goes, "Necessity is the mother of invention," it seems that

---

6. Ibid., 47.
7. From "Fly on the Windscreen" on Depeche Mode's 1986 album *Black Celebration*.

the rise of technological advancements demands that we turn the slogan around. Invention, in our day, is increasingly becoming the mother of necessity, resulting in our focusing solely on the question "Can we?" instead of the more important "Should we?" But if we peel back the layers of mythology that cling to the idea of progress, we quickly discover that we're really going nowhere. Sure, we have more gadgets than we used to, and we can get from point A to point B more quickly than our ancestors could, but we're still in a hurry, and there's still never enough time. Yes, we have made plenty of medical advancements in recent years, but how much of this is merely discovering the ability to cure diseases that our so-called progress caused in the first place? As Ecclesiastes says,

> For everything there is a season, and a time for every matter under heaven: a time to be born, and a time to die; a time to plant, and a time to pluck up what is planted; a time to kill, and a time to heal; a time to break down, and a time to build up; a time to weep, and a time to laugh; a time to mourn, and a time to dance; a time to cast away stones, and a time to gather stones together; a time to embrace, and a time to refrain from embracing; a time to seek, and a time to lose; a time to keep, and a time to cast away; a time to tear, and a time to sew; a time to keep silence, and a time to speak; a time to love, and a time to hate; a time for war, and a time for peace. What gain has the worker from his toil? (3:1–9)

This also is vanity, for time, according to Kreeft, "is just another word for death. Time is a river that takes from us everything it gives us. Nothing remains; time ravages the very stars."[8]

Vanity #4 is evil: "Again I saw all the oppressions that are done under the sun. And behold, the tears of the oppressed, and they had no one to comfort them! On the side of their oppressors there was power, and there was no one to comfort them. . . . There is a vanity that takes place on earth, that there are righteous people to whom it happens according to the deeds of the wicked, and there are wicked people to whom it happens according to the deeds of the righteous. I said that this also is vanity" (Ecc. 4:1, 8:14). The existence of evil is perhaps the most challenging objection to God's existence. If God were good, wouldn't he want to eliminate suffering? If God were powerful, wouldn't he be able to? But suffering exists, meaning that either God is too mean to care or too weak to do anything about it (and in either case, he doesn't make a very compelling case for demanding

---

8. Kreeft, *Three Philosophies*, 48.

our allegiance). "One bull in a china shop, one madman's finger on a machine gun or a nuclear button, one ill-chosen word, one infidelity, can ruin a whole life. Good is hostage to evil. This too is vanity."[9]

The fifth and final example of the vanity and futility of life under the sun may come as a surprise to some, but it is God himself. How can God, the Maker of the world, himself be an example of the world's meaninglessness? The key here is in remembering that the vantage point from which Ecclesiastes surveys our lives is an earthly one, and what's more, it is an earthly one that is divorced from heavenly or eternal concerns. In this context, yes, we can discover that there is a God (for nature itself offers manifold evidence of the existence of an all-wise and all-powerful designer), but that's about as far as mere nature can take us. To put it differently, nature can make God's existence just convincing enough to annoy us; the created order, in other words, can turn us into really irritable theists (and if you stop and think about it, there's nothing more maddening than theism). What we crave is a God who is *here*, not *there*, a God who is more than an absentee landlord or an insignificant other. But that's not the God that Ecclesiastes reveals to us. What it reveals is, paradoxically, the hidden God: "Then I saw all the work of God, that man cannot find out the work that is done under the sun. However much man may toil in seeking, he will not find it out. Even though a wise man claims to know, he cannot find it out. . . . As you do not know the way the spirit comes to the bones in the womb of a woman with child, so you do not know the work of God who makes everything" (8:17; 11:5).

The most significant features of our earthly lives, therefore—the seeming indifference of the universe, death, time, evil, and God—all serve to reinforce the idea that this present world, when considered as an end in itself, reeks of vanity and pointlessness. The question that remains, then, is what are we to do about it?

Cheating at Peek-a-Boo

If Ecclesiastes' conclusion is true that life under the sun is but an unmerry merry-go-round, a wild goose chase without the wild goose, then this fact would seem to be the most gargantuan of "elephants in the room" that we must figure out how to deal with.

9. Ibid., 50.

The Unmerry Merry-Go-Round

It seems to me that there are a few options from which to choose when seeking to come to terms with one's room containing an elephant of this size. One example would be to seek to hide the elephant, perhaps by covering it up with a sheet or something. If that doesn't work, one could always choose to accentuate the elephant with decorations in order to make it blend in with the rest of the room. If this fails, there's always the option of ignoring the elephant altogether. And when that becomes impossible (which it surely must), the only option left would be to simply get used to the idea ("Hello, welcome to our home! Let me take your coat. The bathroom's down the hall—oh *that*? Oh, yes, that's an elephant. We hardly notice it anymore.").

Now I hope the ridiculousness of these examples demonstrates the folly of avoiding to face the claim of Ecclesiastes head-on. What such failure amounts to is what Kreeft calls playing peek-a-boo and refusing to peek. Admittedly, it is easier to bury our head in the sand and hope the problem goes away than it is to face it with open-eyed honesty. But unlike an elephant, which might actually wander off of its own accord, the problem of the vanity of life under the sun isn't going anywhere.

In his book *The Screwtape Letters*, C.S. Lewis offers a fascinating glimpse into the challenges humans face as we seek to navigate these earthly waters and hopefully arrive one day at our heavenly homeland. The book consists of letters written by a fictional demon called Screwtape to his protégé, Wormwood, advising him of the various tactics to employ for the purpose of tempting man and lulling him to sleep, thus distracting him from the destiny of the species. In one letter Screwtape encourages Wormwood concerning the fact that the passage of time can be an ally, since the longer a man lives the more "at home" he feels in the world. Regarding the object of Wormwood's assaults, Screwtape writes:

> But, if only he can be kept alive, you have time itself for your ally. The long, dull, monotonous years of middle-aged prosperity or middle-aged adversity are excellent campaigning weather. You see, it is so hard for these creatures to *persevere*. The routine of adversity, the gradual decay of youthful loves and youthful hopes, the quiet despair (hardly felt as pain) of ever overcoming the chronic temptations with which we have again and again defeated them, the drabness which we create in their lives and the inarticulate resentment with which we teach them to respond to it—all this provides admirable opportunities of wearing out a soul by attrition.

The Destiny of the Species

> If, on the other hand, the middle years prove prosperous, our position is even stronger. Prosperity knits a man to the World. He feels that he is "finding his place in it," while really it is finding its place in him. His increasing reputation, his widening circle of acquaintances, his sense of importance, the growing pressure of absorbing and agreeable work, build up in him a sense of being really at home in earth, which is just what we want.

The arch-demon ends his advice with the unsettling observation: "You will notice that the young are generally less unwilling to die than the middle-aged and the old."[10]

Though this advice is obviously fictional (Lewis wasn't really privy to the counsels of the Underworld), it nonetheless is profound in its insight into the effects that both trials and triumphs have on our earthly lives. When man enters the "long, dull, monotonous years" called middle age, he begins to witness the slow decay of his erstwhile hopefulness and optimism, causing him to be filled with "quiet despair" and "inarticulate resentment" toward the drabness that is now his life. Dave Matthews chillingly captures this attitude in his song "Seek Up," in which he sings:

> *Oh, life it seems*
> *A struggle between*
> *What we see*
> *And what we do.*
> *I'm not going to change my ways*
> *Just to please You, or appease You.*
> *Look at this crowd,*
> *Five billion, proud,*
> *Willing to punch it out;*
> *Right or wrong,*
> *Weak, strong,*
> *Ashes to ashes,*
> *All fall down.*
> *Oh, look around about this—*
> *Around about this*
> *Merry-go-round and around;*
> *Well if at all God's gaze*
> *Upon us falls,*
> *It's with a mischievous grin.*

---

10. Lewis, *The Screwtape Letters*, quoted in *A Year with C.S. Lewis*, 121, emphasis original.

But if man's days are filled not with adversity but with prosperity, says Screwtape, that's even better, for "prosperity knits a man to the world" and makes him "at home in earth." The person being described here is similar to the man of whom Jesus spoke in the Gospels whose possessions became so numerous that his storehouses could no longer contain them, making it necessary for him to build bigger ones. Upon completion, the man was feeling quite smug and self-satisfied. "Soul," the man said to himself, "You are set for life. Eat, drink, and be merry!" But this man's parade was officially rained on when God stepped into the picture and said, "You fool! This very night your soul is required. Now whose will be those possessions you have heaped up for yourself?"[11] As Dave Matthews' song goes on to illustrate, even when we recognize the folly of financial fortitude, that realization still leads to despair when there's nothing to fill that void:

> *Oh, look at me*
> *With my fancy car,*
> *And my bank account.*
> *Oh, how I wish*
> *I could take it all*
> *Down to my grave;*
> *God knows I'd save and save.*
> *Man, take a look again,*
> *Take a look again,*
> *The things you have collected:*
> *In the end it all*
> *Piles up so tall*
> *To one big nothing,*
> *One big nothing at all.*[12]

If we really stop to think about it, cheating at peek-a-boo is rather silly, and the joke's on us.

The Greatest Trick the Devil Ever Pulled. . . .

The objection may be raised at this point which says, "Isn't this all a bit morbid? Calling life farcical and futile just seems a bit over the top. Can't we just enjoy life's simple pleasures without having to worry about ending up as the joke on some sinister hidden camera show that God is staging?"

---

11. This parable is found in Luke 12:13–21. My version is paraphrased.
12. Dave Matthews and Tim Reynolds, *Live at Luther College*, 1999.

Unfortunately for us, we simply cannot go through life in a kind of haze of blissful and enchanted ignorance. If there were ever a time to sit up and pay attention, this would be it. Think about it: If C.S. Lewis is right and there really is an enemy of your soul whose aim is to destroy it, what more effective advice could he give than for us to disregard all this eternity stuff and "enjoy life's simple pleasures"? In other words, although pleasure is a good thing, it can easily become destructive when our affections are disordered and we put earthly things ahead of heavenly ones on our personal priority lists. Consider again Screwtape's counsel to Wormwood concerning how to gain mastery over his subject: "Never forget that when we are dealing with any pleasure in its healthy and normal and satisfying form, we are, in a sense, on the Enemy's (God's) ground . . . it is His invention, not ours. He made the pleasures: all our research so far has not enabled us to produce one. All we can do is to encourage the humans to take the pleasures which our Enemy has produced, at times, or in ways, or in degrees, which He has forbidden."[13] As with the man in Jesus' parable, there is nothing wrong with owning or enjoying possessions *per se*, but when these things become the occasion for inordinate affections that come at the expense of our duly considering the destiny of the species, well, that's when we get ourselves into trouble.

In fact, this is precisely what the Bible is referring to when it speaks about idolatry. To our postmodern ears the concept of idolatry is somewhat quaint—our minds are immediately filled with images of primitive tribespeople chanting and dancing around a statue while a sacrifice is being offered to some god or gods. "What could that possibly have to do with us today? We have *TiVo* and high-speed Internet!"

Going back to Lewis's Screwtape, can we really doubt that, if such a malevolent being exists, and if the Bible does in fact condemn idolatry, the most effective tactic he would employ would involve convincing people with *TiVo* that they are obviously immune from such an ancient practice? After all, what better way to lessen one's resistance to a sin than to give him a false feeling of immunity against it? Such a strategy was surely in the mind of the French poet Baudelaire when he wrote, "The greatest trick the devil ever pulled was convincing the world he doesn't exist." Speaking of the devil's desire for humanity, therefore, Screwtape insists to Wormwood that "an ever-increasing craving for an ever-diminishing pleasure is the

---

13. From *The Screwtape Letters*, quoted in *A Year with C.S. Lewis*, 331.

formula. . . . To get the man's soul and give him nothing in return—that is what really gladdens Our Father's heart."[14]

Is this how we want to end up? Do we really want to play the role of the proverbial pleasure-seeker who can't seem to tear himself away from *American Idol* for long enough to notice that he is lost, that his soul is in ruin, that his life is but a pitiful cliché? Is there anything more pathetic than the person who is so in love with the trifles of this passing age that he refuses to give up what he cannot keep to gain what he cannot lose?

---

14. Ibid.

5

The Earthly Ties That Bind

THUS FAR WE HAVE seen that you and I have a destiny for which we were created, and that we must make the conscious decision to embrace our identity as future-oriented beings and actively seek that destiny out. Failing to do so will only consign us to an earthbound existence characterized by vanity, toil, and ultimately, meaninglessness. What remains to be really investigated, however, are the factors that, when put together, contribute to our failure to live for the future that, deep down, we know we are made for. That's exactly what this chapter will be dedicated to discovering: if we truly are made in God's image with an eternal goal that no temporal pleasures can fulfill, then why, for heaven's sake, don't we immediately embrace it?

The Graffiti of the Gods

"The gods we worship write their names on our faces, be sure of that," wrote Ralph Waldo Emerson. "And a man will worship something—have no doubt about that, either. He may think that his tribute is paid in secret in the dark recesses of his heart—but it will [come] out. That which dominates will determine his life and character. Therefore it behooves us to be careful what we worship, for what we are worshipping, we are becoming."[1] Bob Dylan put it this way a century later:

> *You may be an ambassador to England or France,*
> *You may like to gamble, you might like to dance,*

---

1. Quoted in Stiles, *American Dream*, i.

The Earthly Ties That Bind

> *You may be the heavyweight champion of the world,*
> *You may be a socialite with a long string of pearls . . .*
>
> *But you're gonna have to serve somebody, yes indeed*
> *You're gonna have to serve somebody,*
> *Well, it may be the devil or it may be the Lord*
> *But you're gonna have to serve somebody.*[2]

What both men realized is what we discussed in our previous chapter, namely, that our technological advancements over those primitive people of times long past does little to quench our thirst for idols, and that our identity as divine image-bearers is what lurks behind our need to worship. The problem is that as long as we are opting for the mask instead of our real face, and as long as our affections and priorities are disordered and misdirected, we will always opt for the idol over the real thing.

Jesus told a parable to this effect.[3] There was a father who had two sons, the younger of whom came to him one day and essentially said, "Dad, I've been waiting patiently for my inheritance for many years. But it is becoming increasingly clear to me that the day of your death will never come—is there any way I could, I don't know, have my share of your money now rather than waiting around for you to die?" As insulting as this attitude was on the part of the younger son towards his father, his father acquiesced and divided his possessions between his two boys and gave the younger son what would rightfully be his. In what must have been an even more humiliating act of defiance, this young man then held an "Everything Must Go!" sale and thereby liquidated his father's assets, took the cash, and left town.

After squandering his inheritance on prostitutes and debauchery of various sorts, the younger son then found himself in the midst of a famine with no means of sustenance. He therefore rented himself out as a wage slave to a man who sent him off to tend and feed his pigs. It was at this point that reality set in. "Hmmm," thought the boy, "what does it say about me that I am gazing on the slop that these swine are eating with a sense of mouth-watering envy? Could it be I've taken a misstep somewhere that brought me to this pitiful point?" He then determined to return to his father's house in repentance, humble himself, and ask to be hired on as a servant for whatever the going rate might be. "Though I am no longer worthy to be considered a *son*," thought the boy, "at least his *servants* eat better than

---

2. Bob Dylan, "You Gotta Serve Somebody" from the 1979 album *Slow Train Comin.'*
3. Luke 15:11–32

I have been able to manage lately." In a touching display of forgiveness and restoration, the father cheerfully received the boy back—as a son and not as a servant—proclaiming, "This my son was dead, and he is alive again, he was lost, and now is found!"

While there is a lot in this parable that deserves our attention (such as the picture of God's forgiveness displayed by the father, to which I will return in the next couple chapters), what serves our purpose here is a much simpler and oft-overlooked point. A very basic question could be asked here, namely, why did the younger son leave his father's house? The answer is at once rather complex but quite simple: although there was a tremendous allure on the part of the world that was drawing this young man away from where he truly belonged (with various kinds of pressures and enticements), the fact of the matter is that *the boy left because he wanted to*. Now before you dismiss this point as ridiculously silly and patently obvious, keep in mind what I said in a previous chapter: a man's heart is but a beat ahead of his feet. In other words, wherever your heart's true passion lies, it will only be a matter of time before your feet turn aside to follow those passions (whether your mind wants you to or not). Jesus said it this way: "Do not lay up for yourselves treasures on earth . . . but lay up for yourselves treasures in heaven, where neither moth nor rust destroys and where thieves do not break in and steal. For where your treasure is, there your heart will be also" (Matt. 6:19–21). This is why we are told in the book of Proverbs, "Keep your heart with all vigilance, for from it flow the springs of life" (4:23). What are some of the factors with which our hearts can become entangled as we live in this world, thereby distracting us from our destiny in the next?

The Thickets of the System

In his provocatively-titled book *Is the American Dream Killing You?*, Paul Stiles argues that there is an entity that has usurped an undue influence over the lives of many Americans, employing a complex and web-like system by which it irresistibly draws us in and subjugates us to its demands. In his Prologue, Stiles vividly describes this system by recounting a typical day in the life of a white-collar American man: He wakes up to the sound of a buzzing alarm clock only to be instantly reminded of "the List" containing all the things he failed to accomplish yesterday and which therefore must be done today. He then remembers, while in the shower, that the trash needs to be taken out, and while doing so he can't for the life of him figure out how

The Earthly Ties That Bind

his family manages to produce so much of the stuff (trash cans are much bigger than they were when he was young). Once dressed and shaven, he begins the grueling commute to work (which is a greater challenge than it used to be due to the ever-increasing amount of traffic lights, with their cameras installed by private companies that get a percentage of the money gained by the tickets they help issue). After a quick stop at the McDonald's drive-thru window for coffee (together with a quick glance into the restaurant at the largely-obese clientele), it's time to face the daily bumper-to-bumper freeway commute (this must contribute to today's unhealthy air warning, he thinks). After passing all the ugly, boxy, warehouse-style retail outlets he finally arrives at the office, a full two hours later. After a day consisting of unsatisfying work, he then repeats the commute in reverse, only to arrive home and shovel down some dinner and kiss his already-sleeping kids, watch some news to further depress himself, and then off to bed for his nightly six-hours' rest.

Stiles describes a brief and fleeting moment of clarity on the part of our typical white-collar worker as he falls asleep:

> Why are things this way? The question is so enormous it seems impossible to answer. It goes beyond your country to the very times you live in, to modernity itself. It leads into the very thickets of the system, that ethereal boundary you live in, the invisible source of the way things are, a matrix gone mad. But every once in a while, in rare moments like these when you have a spell of quiet, and feel the presence of your own soul, you sense the answer. There is a common thread connecting the garbage cans to the megahouse, the corporate crime to the selfish government, the income gap to the terrorism . . . the aspirin to Wall Street, the television to the prison population, the stress to the sprawl. Staring into the quiet darkness, you sense that there is something *out there* responsible for this daily insanity, this perpetual chaos, this devastating meaninglessness. There is a reason why nothing makes sense, why life's purpose eludes you, why happiness is so fleeting, why you can't trust anyone anymore, and why so many people around the world would like to see you dead, just because you are an American. There is one primary cause behind this entire psychotic system, and that is—You freeze. No, it can't be! The alarm is ringing.[4]

What Stiles is referring to is what he calls "The Market," and the various chapters of his book document The Market's overbearing influence

---

4. Stiles, *American Dream*, 10–11, emphasis original.

The Destiny of the Species

upon such things as health, the family, reality, the culture, the environment, and the church. In his chapter titled "The Modern God," Stiles insists that every major religion requires its adherents to live a lifestyle that is antithetical to the "Market Code." If we replace the word *moral* with the word *market*—speaking of market values versus moral values or a market society rather than a moral society, for example—we see that these two forces have very different designs: "In each case, moral or market refers to the different end being served, creating two very different sides to life, one Good and the other Productive."[5] He continues:

> In the West, our moral code arises from the Judeo-Christian tradition, where it stems, according to all believers, from a monotheistic God. It is an expression of the innate laws of the human interior, the logic that governs the soul. The Market Code, on the other hand, emerges from Nature, the laws of the physical universe. It is nothing but natural selection in economic guise. This established, early on, a central conflict in our civilization. As Jesus put it, "No man can serve two masters: for either he will hate the one, and love the other; or else he will hold to the one, and despise the other. Ye cannot serve God and mammon."[6]

Stiles chronicles the various ways in which modern people attribute characteristics to the Market that have traditionally been used to describe God. He cites David Loy, who writes:

> Our present economic system should also be understood as our religion, because it has come to fulfill a religious function for us. The discipline of economics is less a science than the theology of that religion, and its god, the Market, has become a vicious circle of ever-increasing production and consumption by pretending to offer a secular salvation. The collapse of the communist "heresy" makes it more apparent that the Market is becoming the first truly world religion, binding all corners of the globe more and more tightly into a world-view and set of values whose religious role we overlook only because we insist on seeing them as "secular."[7]

Harvard theologian Harvey Cox wrote an article for *The Atlantic Monthly* called "The Market as God," in which he argued, "At the apex of

---

5. Ibid., 207, emphasis original.
6. Ibid., 207–08.
7. Loy, "Religion and the Market," quoted in Stiles, *American Dream*, 223.

any theological system, of course, is its doctrine of God. In the new theology this celestial pinnacle is occupied by The Market."[8]

Whether you choose the broader label of The Matrix or the narrower one of The Market matters little. What does matter, though, is that we are surrounded by powers and interests that depend on our allegiance to what Scripture calls "this passing age," and are very threatened when we even consider tearing our gaze away from what is earthly and fixing it on what isn't.

"Waiting Perhaps for a Change of Days"

This idea that there is a malicious intent compelling us to place our allegiance where it ought not be placed is vividly illustrated by that seemingly innocuous piece of jewelry that precipitated what became the age-defining conflict chronicled in Tolkien's *Lord of the Rings* trilogy. The "Ring of Power," as it is called, looked no different from any ordinary ring. But therein lay its subtlety and deceit, for whenever its bearer put it on, it would render him invisible (a benefit useful for all kinds of questionable activities), but it would also begin the slow process of enslaving him and bringing him into subjection to Sauron, the dark lord who originally crafted the Ring. Very few in Tolkien's tale were immune to the Ring's allure, but those who were tempted by it were drawn for various reasons, some external and some internal. The same is true in the spiritual realm for us today. In our next chapter we will consider the internal foothold that causes us to ignore the destiny of the species (a three-letter word beginning with "s" and rhyming with *win*), but here we will continue to restrict our attention to what's outside of us.

In his essay "The Rings of Tolkien and Plato: Lessons in Power, Choice, and Morality," Eric Katz raises the question, "If a mortal being—a human or a hobbit, for example—possesses a Ring of Power, would he choose a moral life?" He continues:

> [I]n this essay I am not primarily concerned with the *physical* aspects of the use of the Ring; I am rather concerned with the *moral* aspects. Does the use of a Ring of Power entail any moral or ethical limits? Is there a morally right or morally wrong way to use a Ring? These questions become even more important when we consider not just any Ring of Power, but the One Ring of Sauron, for the

8. Ibid.

possessor of the One Ring can wield almost unlimited power, and a being who possesses such power would seem to have little reason to concern herself with the dictates of morality.[9]

Katz points out how that the various characters in Tolkien's saga respond to the temptation of the Ring in various ways: Sméagol is utterly consumed by his need for the Ring, eventually (like Merton's "selves" discussed earlier) splitting himself into two distinct personalities: the well-meaning Sméagol he always was, and the malicious creature Gollum, a pale shadow of his former hobbit-like self (Samwise the hobbit refers to these identities as "Slinker" and "Stinker"). Neither wants to see the Ring destroyed or delivered into the hands of Sauron its maker: "Don't take the Precious to Him! . . . Keep it, nice master, and be kind to Sméagol. Don't let Him have it. Or go away, go to nice places, and give it back to little Sméagol. . . . Sméagol will keep it safe; he will do lots of good, especially to nice hobbits."[10] Frodo's response is to point out to his companion that "Already you are being twisted."

The noble warrior Boromir is likewise ensnared, albeit out of an expressed desire to wield the Ring for good, saying to the council that is called to determine what to do with the Ring: "[The Ring] has come into our hands to serve us in the very hour of need. . . . Wielding it the Free Lords of the Free may surely defeat the Enemy. . . . Let the Ring be your weapon. . . . Take it and go forth to victory!"[11] Although he initially acquiesces to the council's rejection of his plea, he eventually succumbs to the Ring's allure and attempts to obtain it by violent force.

Two characters in Tolkien's tale that completely resist the temptation to claim the Ring and use it for themselves are an elf, the Lady Galadriel, and the enigmatic and joyful Tom Bombadil. Galadriel, one of Middle-earth's most powerful rulers, laughs when offered the Ring by Frodo, its bearer (she could easily just take it if she wanted to). Yet, she says, "I do not deny that my heart has greatly desired to ask what you offer." She continues:

> "You will give me the Ring freely! In place of the Dark Lord you will set up a Queen. And I shall not be dark, but beautiful and terrible as the Morning and the Night! Fair as the Sea and the Sun and the Snow upon the Mountain! Dreadful as the Storm and the

---

9. *The Lord of the Rings and Philosophy*, 5, emphasis original.

10. Tolkien, *The Two Towers*, 273, quoted in *The Lord of the Rings and Philosophy*, 9–10.

11. Tolkien, *The Fellowship of the Ring*, 300, quoted in Ibid., 10–11.

The Earthly Ties That Bind

Lightning! Stronger than the foundations of the earth. All shall love me and despair!"

Then she let her hand fall.... She was shrunken: a slender elf-woman, clad in simple white, whose gentle voice was soft and sad. "I pass the test," she said. "I will diminish, and go into the West, and remain Galadriel."[12]

Another character who resisted the Ring's temptation is Tom Bombadil. He is mysterious, for he is neither a wizard nor an elf nor a mortal man (in fact, Tolkien never really explains who or what, exactly, Bombadil is). His wife describes him thusly: "He is, as you have seen him.... He is the Master of wood, water, and hill,"[13] while Bombadil describes himself as "Eldest ... here before the river and the trees."[14] What is especially remarkable about Bombadil is that, at one point in the story, he obtains the Ring from Frodo and puts it on his finger, and it has absolutely no effect on him. He then gives it back as if it were a mere trifle or trinket unworthy of concern.

In seeking to explain the varying effects the Ring has on those who possess it, Katz writes:

> It is clear that Tolkien is demonstrating to us the progressive forces of corruption of the possession and use of the One Ring, for even Frodo, the hero of the book, succumbs to its corruption in his failure to destroy the Ring. He begins with innocent and accidental uses of the Ring's power, but eventually gives over to its seductive power by making conscious and deliberate decisions to wear the Ring, and even, at last, not to destroy it.
>
> [T]he key feature of the corruption caused by the Ring is the corruption of the soul, the "heart," or the personality of the wielder of the Ring. To resist the Ring is to remain oneself, to be the person you are without any extraordinary powers. All who come in contact with the Ring (except, it appears, Bombadil) lose themselves (at least momentarily) in the desire to be greater than they are.[15]

Katz is hinting here at what I referred to above as the "internal foothold" that compels us toward illicit desires (which, as I said, we will look at in detail in our next chapter). What I would like to highlight for our purposes here, though, is the fact that both of the characters who resisted the Ring's power understood themselves to be, for lack of a better word, *above*

---

12. Tolkien, *The Fellowship of the Ring*, 410–11, quoted in Ibid., 12–13.
13. Tolkien, *The Fellowship of the Ring*, 140, quoted in Ibid., 13.
14. Ibid., 13–14.
15. Ibid., 18–19.

the affairs of Middle-earth. Galadriel's true homeland was to be found "in the West," and of Bombadil and the prospect of seeking his counsel, the wizard Gandalf says, "I should not [say that he has a power over the Ring, but] rather that the Ring has no power over him. He is his own master. . . . And now he is withdrawn to a little land, within bounds that he has set, though none can see them, waiting perhaps for a change of days, and he will not step beyond them." When asked whether the Ring can be entrusted to Bombadil and kept within his realm, Gandalf replies, "He would not understand the need. And if he were given the Ring, he would soon forget it, or most likely throw it away. Such things have no hold on his mind."[16]

Swinging the discussion to our investigation of the destiny of the species, it is not simply the case that one needs a lack of attachment to this world in order to resist its allure. We all live in this world, we breathe its air, we enjoy its art, and we partake of its fruits. No amount of mystical detachment can ever be achieved that would inoculate us against our present earthly context. "Then why bring up the examples of Galadriel and Bombadil?," you may be asking. My point is to highlight, not their detachment from this age, but their attachment to another one—not their hatred of the temporal, but their love for what is eternal.

It is the same with us. The life God calls us to, despite the impression given by some of his followers, is not a solely negative one that is characterized by asceticism and denial of all things physical.[17] No, coupled with every disincentive *from* something is an alternate incentive *toward* something else. Just as Tom Bombadil was "waiting perhaps for a change of days," so we who have come to discover and embrace the destiny of the species are sufficiently drawn by what's ahead of us that we refuse to be driven by what lies behind. As I argued in chapter 1, we are not pushed, but pulled (which is precisely what makes us human).

Frustration Misdirected

It is here where things can get complicated. Plenty of people in our day are indeed disgruntled with earth and its present state of affairs, but their various solutions, while often attractive, miss the point entirely. In David Sirota's insightful book *The Uprising*, the author tells the story of "the populist revolt scaring Wall Street and Washington." The blurb on the inside cover

---

16. Tolkien, *The Fellowship of the Ring*, 279.
17. For a more detailed discussion of this, see Stellman, *Dual Citizens*.

reads: "Job outsourcing. Perpetual busy signals at government agencies. Slashed paychecks. Stolen elections. A war without end, fatally mismanaged. Ordinary Americans on both the Right and Left are tired of being disenfranchised by corrupt politicians of both parties and are organizing to change the status quo. In his invigorating new book, David Sirota investigates whether this uprising can be transformed into a unified, lasting political movement."[18] Sirota surveys everything from the offices of progressive third party political candidates to the front lines of the ultraconservative Minutemen's struggle along the Mexican border, demonstrating how many Americans—regardless of their political leanings—are fed up with the status quo.

A similar approach is taken by *Rolling Stone*'s Matt Taibbi in his book *The Great Derangement*, in which he goes undercover in order to infiltrate such diverse sectors of society as American military bases in Baghdad, the U.S. Congress, the meetings of 9/11 conspiracy theorists, and the Christian megachurch in order to understand and report on the sense of disillusionment and disenfranchisement that drives people to such extreme expressions of frustration about the way things are.[19]

My point is not to dismiss activism or encourage lethargy, but to remind us that it is not enough to be sufficiently disenchanted with earth so that we set out to simply make it a bit better. Don't get me wrong, I think "We Are the World" is a good song and all, but we mustn't kid ourselves into thinking that being "the ones to make a brighter day" will quench our thirst for the eternal Day that will not merely be a bit brighter than we're used to, but will blaze with the very glory of God's loving presence. Simply put, as much as we all may welcome a new and improved earth, our efforts to achieve it are often examples of a misdirected longing, a correct desire with an incorrect object.

If Emerson was correct about our becoming what we worship, and if Jesus' words are true that wherever we ultimately place our treasure is where our hearts will lead us, then it simply couldn't be more crucial that we resist the allure of this age to capitulate to its demands, to subject ourselves to its trends, and to heed its false and deadly promises.

---

18. Sirota, *The Uprising*.
19. Taibbi, *The Great Derangement*.

6

Sin (Yes, That Word Still Exists)

As lovers of well-written comedy, my wife and I never miss an episode of NBC's Emmy-winning program *30 Rock*. A kind of "show within a show," *30 Rock* centers around a fictional sketch comedy program similar to *Saturday Night Live*, with its main characters being the writers, actors, and executives whose job it is to air the show on a weekly basis. The character who steals the show, in my opinion, is Jack Donaghy (played by Alec Baldwin), an NBC exec known for his straight-laced, right wing conservatism. In one particular scene, he compliments one of his female underlings on a shrewd observation, saying, "You know, you'd make a good businessman." When she replies, "You mean, 'business*woman*,'" Donaghy retorts with complete seriousness, "I don't think that's a word."

Many people today exhibit a similar reaction when the subject of *sin* arises. Perhaps you have been the target of the evangelistic efforts of a well-meaning Christian who told you that "All have sinned, and fall short of the glory of God" (Rom. 3:23), and you thought to yourself, "*Sinned*? What is this, a Shakespeare play or something? Look, I like the Dark Ages as much as the next guy, but let's be honest, the concept is a tad antiquated." In other words, when you hear the word "sin" it has the same effect as "businesswoman" does upon Jack Donaghy: the very idea just fails to register. In this chapter I hope to restore the concept of sin to a place of relevance in the minds of those for whom the idea just seems silly. It is against the backdrop of darkness that light truly shines, after all, and good news never sounds all that good without the bad news preceding it.

Sin (Yes, That Word Still Exists)

Ain't That a Shame?

I doubt that any thinking person with his ear to the ground would question the statement that sin, and the sense of shame that once resulted from it, has largely disappeared from American society. To give one humorous example of just how outdated these concepts are, consider the satirical newspaper *The Onion*'s article titled "Grandmother Classifies 79% of Everything a Shame":

> SANDUSKY, OH—According to those close to Gertrude Wharton, the grandmother of nine declares 79 percent of everything she witnesses, experiences, or hears about from friends to be "a shame."
>
> Though Wharton, 83, has proclaimed things to be a shame in the past, her current usage of the word has been a growing cause for concern. Witnesses report that in the past 24 hours alone she has applied the term to a fallen tree, a graduation card to a grandchild that arrived late, and a news story about a golf course. Several times a day, loved ones say, she shakes her head and declares the event or statement that most recently came up in conversation to be "a shame," and then a soulful, knowing look comes into her eyes, often accompanied by a sigh.
>
> "I remember her saying it when we were growing up," granddaughter Danielle Treece said. "But it was usually when she was trying to make us feel better about something. It was kind of cute. Now she's saying it about the lightbulb that burned out in the hallway. I'm like, 'Grandma, I'll change it. It's fine,' but no matter what it is we're talking about, she acts like she just found out Hitler invaded Poland or something."[1]

Satire aside, a more serious commentary on the antiquated nature of shame was given in a 1995 *Newsweek* article titled "The Return of Shame: Americans Are Fed Up With Everything From Teen Pregnancy To Drunk Drivers. How Do We Restore A Sense Of Right And Wrong?"[2] The piece begins: "A 16-year-old Maryland boy who is serving time in a juvenile-detention center for sexually molesting his 9-year-old sister wants to go home. But before Montgomery County court officials will release him, the boy must convince his family that he feels an emotion that for decades has been either scorned as destructive to self-esteem or dismissed as hopelessly

---

1. http://www.theonion.com/articles/grandmother-classifies-79-of-everything-a-shame,2769/.

2. http://www.newsweek.com/id/106370.

old-fashioned. He must prove that he feels a sense of shame." How positively medieval, right? But wait, there's more:

> In this case, showing that he is ashamed means not just admitting his crime and apologizing to his sister, but literally getting down on his knees. The kneeling is only one part of a lengthy rehabilitation process, but if the boy doesn't comply in a heartfelt way, he can't go home and the case will be sent back to county authorities. "They need to understand that what they did was so bad that they must get into a body posture that says 'repentance'—the words are not enough," says Cloe Madanes, director of the Family Therapy Institute in Rockville, Md. Her colleague James Keim adds: "In our society, we use the same words—'I'm sorry'—to apologize for raping your daughter as we do for spilling milk. It's the physical gesture that makes the difference."

I trust we all can appreciate just how contrary to our culture's thinking this kind of thing really is. Sure, the practice of kneeling and confessing one's sins isn't all that revolutionary for many churchgoers, but let's be honest, there are becoming increasingly fewer of those around anymore.

It is no accident that our society's cavalier attitude about sin coincides with an increasingly cavalier attitude about God. Despite the efforts of many to retain traditional moral norms while simultaneously dismissing God's existence as a pious myth, the fact is that without a holy and transcendent Being to ground human morality, the very concept begins to come apart at the seams. Think about it: if there is no God, then there can be no basis for saying that some seemingly-heinous act is objectively wrong. Take 9/11 as an example. Most people see the events of that day as a horrific crime against humanity, and their viewpoint is rooted in the idea that it is wrong to kill innocent people. But who says it's wrong to kill innocent people? Just because most societies agree on this ethical point doesn't mean that the terrorists who highjacked those planes have to conform to it, right? What if their particular society thinks it's perfectly OK to kill people who don't share their worldview, who are we to judge? After all, if there is no one or nothing bigger than us, who stands outside of us with the ability to judge us, then all we are left with is the evolutionary principle of the survival of the fittest. And that, my dear readers, is a really ineffective principle for dissuading people from engaging in atrocious behavior.

Now the objection could easily arise, "But the 9/11 terrorists did what they did *not* because of their atheism, but because of their theism!" This is true: it was their warped and misguided understanding of God that caused them to do what they did. But this is merely the exception that proves the rule. After all, just because a person or group acts inconsistently with the principles they claim to hold doesn't disprove the principles themselves, only the faithfulness of the ones holding them. And moreover, without God's existence we would be in no position to be able to recognize how utterly inconsistent such God-professing terrorists are. In other words, the only way we can recognize religious hypocrisy for what it is, is by evaluating it in the light of the objective morality for which God's existence provides the basis.

There's really no way around it. As difficult to accept as the concept of sin may be, it is grounded in the existence of a holy God, the same God whose existence grounds our ability to determine right from wrong, whose existence establishes our ability to recognize what is good and distinguish it from what is evil, and whose existence provides us with somewhere to direct our prayers when we recognize how fortunate we are and just need Someone to thank.

Congratulations, You're Better Than Hitler!

We have seen thus far how foreign the concept of sin is to our supposedly enlightened and postmodern culture, it now remains for us to roll up our sleeves and consider what sin actually is.

As we have touched upon already, the idea of sin only makes sense if there is some objective standard against which human behavior can be judged, a set of cosmic scales in which our thoughts and actions can be weighed. And as we've also seen, unless we want to reduce all moral determinations to mere judgment-calls (saying that 9/11 or the Holocaust were only evil *in our opinion*), then such a standard—and the God whose existence grounds that standard—must exist outside of us. Now taking our logic a step further, if the vast majority of humans, despite the differences in their religious expression, agree on the basics of what constitutes good and bad behavior (as in, helping people *good*, murdering people *bad*), then it would seem to follow that the God who provides the basis for these determinations is himself a good Being. In fact, it would make sense to say that he is the original Archetype of goodness, because of whom we can recognize good behavior when we see it, and without whom we could not recognize evil when it presents itself. So to sum up where we've come thus far, the very fact that we call some things "good" and others "evil" demonstrates a moral awareness that atheism cannot explain, but which theism can.

Now it is true that plenty of Americans will not object to this idea that there's someone or something out there looking out for the good guys and seeking to punish the bad ones. Many are agnostic, but are open to the idea that God exists, and many others are theists who have determined that he does. But it is crucial that we not stop here, for bare theism will do none of us any good at the end of the day. The temptation is always present (especially for mere theists) to define "God" in such a way as to make him eerily similar to one's self. "God," in other words, approves of everything I approve of and is annoyed with everything that irritates me. His attitude is incredibly gracious toward my sins, but he can't tolerate the flaws in others. Isn't it an uncanny coincidence that he and I are so similar? I mean, what are the chances that the God I worship loves Fox News, wants to liberate Iraqis, *and* wants to keep Mexicans out of California? We think so alike, it's almost like we're the same person!

Well, in cases like this, it is often true that "God" and the worshiper *are* the same person, for the former was actually invented by the latter, with man creating God in his own image and according to his own likeness (rather than the other way around). Remember what we saw earlier: idolatry is not just for naked tribesmen dancing around totem poles, it is committed by all who fashion a god to suit their own desires and reinforce their own opinions. Paul the apostle put it this way:

> For the wrath of God is revealed from heaven against all ungodliness and unrighteousness of men, who by their unrighteousness suppress the truth. For what can be known about God is plain to them, because God has shown it to them. For his invisible attributes, namely, his eternal power and divine nature, have been clearly perceived, ever since the creation of the world, in the things that have been made. So they are without excuse. For although they knew God, they did not honor him as God or give thanks to him, but they became futile in their thinking, and their foolish hearts were darkened. Claiming to be wise, they became fools . . . because they exchanged the truth about God for a lie and worshiped and served the creature rather than the Creator, who is blessed forever! Amen (Rom. 1:18–22, 25).

According to Paul in this passage, despite the fact that all people can see clear evidence of God's existence and learn something of his character as they examine the created order, our natural inclination is to respond to

Sin (Yes, That Word Still Exists)

this evidence by suppressing it. Rather than worship and serve the Creator, he says, we choose to direct our attention to that which is created, whether these idols be crafted of wood or stone, or made with microchips or V8 engines (and of course, our idols can be less tangible than this, taking the form of our careers, stock portfolios, and even ourselves).

One of the primary characteristics of idolatry is to cause those who commit it to define sin in a strictly self-serving way. The way this often works is by inventing a god who sees the sins of those who irritate us as potentially damning, while looking at our own sins as mere minor faults or character flaws that don't really matter all that much. The label of "sinful," accordingly, is always applied to those who are slightly worse than we, but never to ourselves. Jesus, in the context of his admonition to "Judge not, that you be not judged" (the only verse in the Bible that many people seem to know), spoke of the man who obsesses over the speck of sawdust in his brother's eye while ignoring the two-by-four in his own. What is particularly interesting about this saying is the fact that the two foreign substances are made of the same material, thus indicating that we are often especially sensitive to the sins of others that are similar to the ones we struggle with (and are often willing to condemn much milder expressions of those sins in others than we are the more serious eruptions of them in our own lives).

A fitting example of this is seen in the life of King David. Though he began his kingly reign as "a man after God's own heart," there came a point in his life when he fell into temptation and sin, committing adultery with his neighbor's wife, and then having her husband deliberately killed in battle to cover up the offense. After keeping his sin a secret for many months, David was finally visited by Nathan the prophet and told a story about a rich man who had many flocks and herds but who, when entertaining guests at his house, chose to steal his neighbor's pet lamb to slaughter and serve to his friends instead of killing one from his numerous flocks. Filled with hypocritical anger, the king (who may have thought that the prophet was presenting him with an actual case for adjudication) cried out not only for the rich man to restore fourfold to his neighbor (which is what God required in his law), but also for his blood to be shed for his offense. Interesting, is it not, that David can so easily sentence a man to death for what was not even a capital crime, while failing to repent of his own transgressions, which were similar in nature but infinitely more serious? As we would expect, David's cry "This man shall surely die!" was answered by Nathan's retort "*You* are the man!," which thankfully occasioned the king's humble repentance and his penning of the fifty-first Psalm, arguably the most beautiful and sublime expression of contrition and brokenness of heart in all of Scripture.

When we come to realize that sin is more than our own personal list of the aggravating things that people do to annoy us, but is in fact *any* violation of the law of God—which is itself an expression of his holy character—no matter how small or seemingly insignificant, we will finally see our sin for what it is. Perhaps an illustration would be helpful. A little girl looks out her bedroom window and sees a sheep eating grass. "Wow, look how white that sheep is!," she says. But then it begins to snow, and after the ground is covered she again looks at the sheep and exclaims, "Wow, look how dirty that sheep is!" What happened to change the girl's assessment of the sheep's cleanness? Did the sheep fall in the mud? Did the girl simply misspeak the first time? No, and no. In both cases we have the exact same sheep, but what changed is the backdrop against which the sheep's color is judged. When compared with the green grass, the sheep indeed looked clean and white. But when the backdrop shifted to freshly-fallen snow, the very same sheep suddenly didn't appear white at all, but dirty.

The same principle applies to us today. As long as we insist on comparing ourselves with others, it will be impossible to gain a valid moral assessment of ourselves. "Sure," we say, "we all make mistakes (I mean, nobody's perfect, right?). But come on, I'm not as bad as Hitler or anything, so on judgment day (if there really is such a thing) I should be fine." I trust you can see the problem with this line of thinking: with very few exceptions, every person can find someone else who is worse than he himself is, thus enabling us to grade on a huge curve and inevitably pass our own test by rigging the game from the get-go. But when the standard against which we will be judged ceases to be fluid, ever-changing, and always worse than we are, but rather is the law of God which perfectly expresses his holy nature, the game suddenly ceases to look as easily winnable as it once did.

And let's be honest: the inspired author of the biblical Proverbs, the ancient Greek moral philosophers, and America's own virtuous figures such as "Honest Abe" Lincoln and Martin Luther King would probably turn over in their graves if they knew that our twenty-first-century standard of morality consisted of merely being better than Hitler. Talk about lowering the bar . . . .

Sin (Yes, That Word Still Exists)

We Fought the Law, but the Law Won

Well, we can't continue merely alluding to God's law without actually dusting off those stone tablets and examining what it is they demand of us, can we? I realize that the prospect of looking at all ten commandments is a potential recipe for a chapter half-read, but trust me, most people (perhaps you yourself) are tragically unaware of what the law actually says. Sure, cultural conservatives can huff and puff until they're blue in the face when a liberal judge orders the Decalogue to be removed from public buildings, saying things like, "America is a Christian nation! How can we just flush our religious heritage down the toilet?" But when you ask such religious patriots to name the ten commandments, the response is often something like, "Well, you know: 'Thou shalt not kill,' 'Thou shalt not commit adultery,' umm, 'Don't lie,' 'Be a good neighbor.' There's, uh, the one about 'early to bed, early to rise,' and then the thing about 'fighting fire with fire.' Oh, and 'to thine own self be true.'" Yes, the first three are actual commandments, but the source of the rest is anywhere from Ben Franklin, Mister Rogers, Shakespeare, or Metallica. My point? You probably don't know the commandments as well as you think you do (so maybe skipping ahead is a bad idea).

The first four commands deal with our vertical relationship with God, and the last six deal with our horizontal relationship with our fellow men and women.[3] The law begins with, "I am the LORD your God . . . you shall have no other gods before Me," and the second says, "You shall not make for yourself a carved image, or any likeness of anything . . . . You shall not bow down to them or serve them, for I the LORD your God am a jealous God . . . ." Here we see the official condemnation of the practice of idolatry that we have discussed already. As we have noted, idolatry can be committed by anyone—ancient, modern, or postmodern—who allows anyone or anything to take the place in their lives and affections that belongs to God alone. Whatever it is that consumes our thoughts and elicits our devotion, whether we admit it or not, is God to us, and the real God who made us for himself will suffer no rival to his throne.

The third commandment is "You shall not take the Name of the LORD your God in vain." This command not only prohibits the blaspheming of God's Name (which we commit every time we substitute "God" or "Jesus" for a common curse word), but it also has a positive function, requiring

---

3. The ten commandments can be found in Exodus 20 and Deuteronomy 5.

that whenever we speak or think the Name of God, we do so with all the reverence and honor that his holy Name deserves. In Scripture there is always a profound connection between a person and his or her name, and this is no less true when it comes to God. If his Name reflects his character, then it ought to be used with the utmost care and respect, for as God says at the end of the third commandment, "The LORD will not hold him guiltless who takes his Name in vain."

If the first three commandments focused on whom man ought to worship, and how, the fourth concerns the when: "Remember the Sabbath day, to keep it holy." For Israel before the coming of Christ, it was the seventh day of the week (Saturday) that was to be set aside for worship and rest from non-holy labors, while for us today it is the first day of the week (Sunday) that we are to use for the purpose of gathering with God's people for worship.[4] Laying aside all of the technical and theological considerations that could arise here, suffice it to say that for most Americans, setting aside an entire day in seven for the sole purpose of worshiping God with his people, for reading and hearing his Word, for singing his praises, for meditating upon his goodness, and for seeking his face, is altogether unheard of and, in the minds of many, completely unrealistic and unworkable. "You don't understand," we often hear (from believers and non-believers alike), "I have a family and a lot of responsibilities and pressure. On Saturdays I run errands and get things done around the house, and on Sundays I catch up on some last-minute stuff and, hopefully, watch the ballgame." While I certainly understand just how foreign the idea of corporate worship and Sabbath-keeping sounds in the ears of most non-churchgoers, if we stop and consider it a moment, I think we will conclude that giving a mere day out of each week to the God who both created and desires to redeem us is not exactly a tall order.

The fifth commandment says, "Honor your father and mother." Setting aside all the potential objections to this rule, the fact remains that there is something so obviously right about showing honor and deference not only to our parents, but also to all in authority over us, whether bosses, police, or civil magistrates. A mere glance at certain reality TV shows only reinforces how far we've fallen from the days when parents and other authority figures were treated with the respect to which their positions entitle them.

---

4. For an in-depth discussion of the fourth commandment, see Stellman, *Dual Citizens*, 51–62.

Sin (Yes, That Word Still Exists)

Next is "You shall not kill." Now before you shout, "Yes! Finally one I've actually kept," you should be aware of just how deep and penetrating this command really is. The point of this command is not merely to get us to refrain from physically murdering people, but it also governs our inward attitudes towards those whom we dislike. Listen to how Jesus himself taught the sixth commandment: "You have heard that it was said to those of old, 'You shall not murder; and whoever murders will be liable to judgment.' But I say to you that everyone who is angry with his brother will be liable to judgment; whoever insults his brother will be liable to the council; and whoever says, 'You fool!' will be liable to the hell of fire" (Matt. 5:21–22). So much for Jesus being the kinder, gentler version of Moses, the good cop to the Old Testament God's bad cop! According to his explanation, we can break the sixth commandment by the hatred we have in our hearts, before we ever lift a finger to actually harm anyone.

A similar principle is at work with the seventh commandment, which says, "You shall not commit adultery." On this command Jesus says,

> "You have heard that it was said, 'You shall not commit adultery.' But I say to you that everyone who looks at a woman with lustful intent has already committed adultery with her in his heart. If your right eye causes you to sin, tear it out and throw it away. For it is better that you lose one of your members than that your whole body be thrown into hell. And if your right hand causes you to sin, cut it off and throw it away. For it is better that you lose one of your members than that your whole body go into hell" (Matt. 5:27–30).

Again, it appears that Jesus is concerned with far more than merely our outward conduct. As the prophet Samuel said, "God does not see as man sees, for man looks on the outward appearance, but God looks on the heart" (I Sam. 16:7). Every idle thought or lustful intent that we inwardly entertain will testify against us on the day of judgment, crying out for our condemnation.

The eighth commandment is, "You shall not steal," which sounds relatively un-alarming until we ask the simple question, "How much does one have to steal to be a thief?" Would a paperclip or a box of pens from the office supply room suffice? Or does God not count little infractions like this since they don't come up to the monetary qualification that we arbitrarily tack on to this command? To hit perhaps even closer to home, should what we Americans call "good business" actually be classified as theft from God's perspective? Consider the words of James:

> Come now, you rich, weep and howl for the miseries that are coming upon you. Your riches have rotted and your garments are moth-eaten. Your gold and silver have corroded, and their corrosion will be evidence against you and will eat your flesh like fire. You have laid up treasure in the last days. *Behold, the wages of the laborers who mowed your fields, which you kept back by fraud, are crying out against you*, and the cries of the harvesters have reached the ears of the Lord of hosts. You have lived on the earth in luxury and in self-indulgence. You have fattened your hearts in a day of slaughter (Jas. 5:1–5, emphasis added).

Technical and highly-nuanced discussions of capitalism aside, it is at least worth asking whether the hallowed practice of a company's paying its employees as little as possible to manufacture goods that can be sold for as much as possible is both immoral, and a violation of the eighth commandment.

The ninth commandment says, "You shall not bear false witness." In addition to prohibiting lying, slander, libel, gossip, and backbiting, this command requires that we speak and promote the truth and defend the good name of our neighbor. During Jesus' trial, Pontius Pilate asked, "What is truth?" In John's account of Christ's ministry, Jesus claimed, "*I am the Truth*," and in Matthew's gospel he warned, "I tell you, on the day of judgment people will give account for every careless word they speak, for by your words you will be justified, and by your words you will be condemned" (12:36–37). Sure, we love to euphemize our lies as "white lies" or "half-truths," but that's the thing about euphemism and spin: it's just another form of lying (and if you think about it, coming up with euphemisms for lying is a tad ironic, don't you think?).

The last of the ten commandments states, "You shall not covet . . . anything that is your neighbor's." Antiquated language aside, this commandment expressly forbids what we often call "keeping up with the Joneses," the characteristic American obsession with accumulating more and more stuff.[5] A famous singer once summed up the difference between the American attitude toward fame and prosperity with that of his own countrymen. "When an American looks up at the mansion on the hill, he encourages himself by saying, 'One day, I'm going to have that life.' When someone in my country looks up at the mansion on the hill, he encourages himself by saying, 'One day, that guy's gonna crash and burn!'" The tenth

---

5. On this topic, see Stiles, *American Dream*, and Schor, *The Overspent American*.

Sin (Yes, That Word Still Exists)

commandment forbids both of these attitudes, demanding that we rejoice at the prosperity of others rather than becoming envious of it.

We've Lost That Guilty Feeling

How are we to respond to this information? Are we to use God's law as a means to measure how well we've performed? You may be patting yourself on the back for only having violated five out of 10, thinking, "Not too shabby, and with a little more effort I'll be batting a thousand!" The problem, however, is that this isn't baseball, and God doesn't grade on a curve. As I have mentioned already, God's law is not an arbitrary standard that he invented so that he could have an excuse to be mad at us. Rather, it is an expression of his very nature and character, which are infinitely holy and pure. "God is light," writes John, "and in him is no darkness at all" (I John 1:5), and Isaiah is even more bold: "For behold, the LORD will come in fire, and his chariots like the whirlwind, to render his anger in fury, and his rebuke with flames of fire. For by fire will the LORD enter into judgment, and by his sword, with all flesh; and those slain by the LORD shall be many" (66:15–16). The reason for this future judgment is that God, if he is to be a just Judge, must by definition must punish sin and right all wrongs. In the same way that a human judge cannot simply turn a blind eye to evil, so much more impossible is it for God to do so.

In seeking to determine our appropriate response to the knowledge that we have violated God's law and exposed our guilty souls to his relentlessly penetrating judgment, consider the following illustration: a young boy is playing ball in the house. At a certain point he loses control of the ball and it knocks over a vase that his father had warned him many times never to touch, or even go near. As the vase shatters into a million pieces, the boy is gripped with horror. A moment later, however, he remembers seeing an identical vase in a local department story with a price-tag of $2.00. Realizing that he had overreacted to the seriousness of his mistake, the boy says to his father when he gets home from work, "Hey, I broke that vase thingy, but it's no problem, I can buy another one with my own money. Just deduct the $2.00 from my weekly allowance." The father turns white as a ghost and walks over to his son, places his hands on the boy's shoulders, and says, "Son, that was no cheap imitation vase, it was an antique valued at $20,000! It will take everything I've got, but I will replace it myself." At that moment, as tears fill his eyes, the boy at last understands the seriousness of

The Destiny of the Species

what he has done. Needless to say, his love and gratitude toward his father grew greater than ever before from that moment on.

What was it that caused the boy to appreciate the grave significance of his crime? Was it not his realization of the vase's value to his father? As long as he thought it was a cheap vase that could easily be replaced with a couple bucks-worth of allowance money, why bother getting all worked up or remorseful about it? No harm, no foul, right? But once he realized that there was nothing he could do to restore what he, in his foolishness, had broken, and that the only way to replace the shattered vase was for his father to incur the cost himself, he was able to exhibit the kind of grief and contrition that an infraction of that magnitude truly demanded.[6]

Turning our attention once again to our own spiritual situation, as long as we entertain shallow and cavalier attitudes about our own plight (thinking that the divine law which we have shattered into a million pieces can be replaced by a couple dollars' worth of our own moral efforts at self-improvement), we will never display the appropriate sorrow for sin that our crimes necessitate. Despite the encouragement of many so-called Christian evangelists to stop being so negative, to stop dwelling so morbidly on our sin, and to move past all the guilt so that we can start to "become better us-es," the fact is that, biblically speaking, it is always the *false* prophets who "heal the wound superficially, saying 'Peace! Peace!' when there is no peace" (Jer. 6:14). In the same way that sick patients appreciate the candidness of their doctor as he lays out the seriousness of their disease, when we are dealing with a sickness-of-soul that is far more dire than any physical malady, we need to be able to face the problem head on. Although the truth (in both cases) is never easy to hear, it is always preferable to candy-coated placebos and trite spiritual slogans.

If James was correct when he said that breaking one of God's commands renders us guilty of breaking them all, then the sooner we appreciate the danger to which we have exposed our guilty souls, the sooner we will begin to treat the destiny of the species as more than merely a nice, pious pipedream according to which we'll all join hands and sing "It's a Small World" for all eternity. Although the heavenly end for which God made us ought to be our goal, the divine law stands like a firing squad consisting of ten massive cannons that will pronounce its sentence upon all whose sin has not been dealt with. We will discuss God's remedy in a subsequent chapter, but for now, perhaps it is best that you close this book and take

---

6. I am indebted to Ray Comfort for providing this illustration.

your own spiritual temperature, examining yourself in the light of God's holy demands.

7

From Eternity to Here

If it is true that there is a seemingly insurmountable hurdle that is blocking our way to fulfilling the destiny of the species—that hurdle being *sin*, as we saw in our last chapter—then the question we must now deal with is, "How can this hurdle be cleared?" If sin is truly a deal-breaker, then is God's entire project a sham, nothing but a cosmic abortion, an example of wonderful intentions that never really got off the ground? In this chapter we will seek to determine how it is that mankind's eternal destiny can be fulfilled in spite of our sinful and fallen condition. Before we answer the question, however, we must appreciate just how serious a dilemma this really is.

Dead in Sin

As we saw in our last chapter, every single one of us has sinned and broken God's law, and thus have rendered ourselves guilty before his heavenly tribunal. But what does this mean? How exactly has our sin affected us? Depressing as it may sound to our culture's ears (obsessed as many of us are with youth, cheerfulness, and Justin Bieber), the metaphor that the Bible employs to describe our spiritual condition is that of *death*. Consider what Paul says to the church in Ephesus: "And you were dead in the trespasses and sins in which you once walked, following the course of this world, following the prince of the power of the air, the spirit that is now at work in the sons of disobedience—among whom we all once lived in the passions of our flesh, carrying out the desires of the body and the mind, and were by nature children of wrath, like the rest of mankind" (Eph. 2:1–3). The Bible's use of the metaphor of death is not tricky theological wordplay, nor does understanding it require an advanced degree in divinity. It's pretty simple, actually: in the same way that a physically dead person is incapable of doing anything to remedy his physical condition, so a spiritually dead person is equally incapable of doing anything to remedy his spiritual condition. Having watched my share of *ER*, I think I have learned a thing or two about the practice of medicine, and have even gained the expertise to know that when medics are called to the scene of an accident, they need to do a lot more than just passively encourage someone whose heart has stopped beating to get up and walk it off. No, such advice is useless, especially when the victim has already died.

When it comes to our spiritual condition, we are all by nature "dead in sin" and therefore unable to remedy our own plight. While God's law does indeed promise blessings to the one who keeps it, the fact is that none of us has done so. Most people, of course, are not nearly as bad as they might be if they completely rid themselves of all their inhibitions and just did whatever they felt like doing. But even our occasional self-restraint will not save us. Paul writes to the Romans, citing the Jewish Scriptures:

> What then? Are we Jews any better off [than others]? No, not at all. For we have already charged that all, both Jews and Greeks, are under sin, as it is written:
>
>> "None is righteous, no, not one;
>> no one understands;
>> no one seeks for God.
>> All have turned aside; together they have become worthless;
>> no one does good,
>> not even one."
>> "Their throat is an open grave;
>> they use their tongues to deceive."
>> "The venom of asps is under their lips."
>> "Their mouth is full of curses and bitterness."
>> "Their feet are swift to shed blood;
>> in their paths are ruin and misery,
>> and the way of peace they have not known."
>> "There is no fear of God before their eyes."
>
> Now we know that whatever the law says it speaks to those who are under the law, so that every mouth may be stopped, and the whole world may be held accountable to God. For by works of the law no human being will be justified in his sight, since through the law comes knowledge of sin (3:10–19)

It is clear from this passage that one of the primary purposes of God's law is *not* to demonstrate how good we are, but just the opposite: to demonstrate how bad we are.

Part of what it means to be dead in sin is that we cannot get ourselves out of the hole we've dug. According to the Bible, we cannot simply choose to do better or decide to save ourselves. In fact, Jesus went so far as to say that even trusting in Him is beyond our natural ability since we are fallen by nature: "No one can come to Me unless the Father who sent Me draws him" (John 6:44).

What are we to make of this supposed inability? Is it really the case that even something as simple as obeying God's command to trust in Jesus to save us is beyond our capacity to perform? I can hear the objection already: "So you're really telling me I can't decide to become a Christian if I want to? But of course I can! I do have free will, you know!" It is important at this point to understand exactly what the Bible means when it tells us that certain things are beyond our capacity to choose. No one is denying that we all have the ability to make choices, and that we do so every single day. Nor do we deny that we often (perhaps even always) choose what we want. Ah, but therein lies the problem! Man's dilemma is not that he can't choose what he wants, but that he can and does. In other words, because we are sinful and fallen, it is only natural for us to choose what is sinful rather than what is holy. In the same way that I would never go to a restaurant and order Brussels sprouts even if I were given the choice to do so a million times, so we sinful men and women will never exercise our free wills to choose to repent and trust in Christ unless God the Father inwardly moves us by first softening our hearts and opening our eyes to see the truth of the gospel.

To the Rescue!

Given our fallen condition, in order for God's purpose for us to be fulfilled a Rescuer needed to come on the scene and undo the mess we had gotten ourselves into. One of the fathers of the early church, Gregory of Nyssa, wrote the following in c. 372 A.D.: "Sick, our nature demanded to be healed; fallen, to be raised up; dead, to rise again. We had lost the possession of the good; it was necessary for it to be given back to us. Closed in the darkness, it was necessary to bring us the light; captives, we awaited a Savior; prisoners, help; slaves, a liberator. Are these things minor or insignificant? Did they

From Eternity to Here

not move God to descend to human nature and visit it, since humanity was in so miserable and unhappy a state?"[1] That last sentence may have caused you to pause and scratch your head in astonishment (at least it should have, you may need to have a second look): Did not man's predicament, asks Gregory, move God to *descend to human nature*? What exactly was this ancient saint getting at? He must have meant simply that God would snap his divine fingers from his throne and work some magical hocus-pocus, and thereby save us, right? I mean, he's *God*, how much trouble would he really go to in order to bring about a solution to our plight?

According to Christianity, much more than we often dare to imagine. The Bible teaches that the second Person of the Holy Trinity, the divine Son of God, assumed a human nature along with his divine nature in order to be our Champion and Savior, thereby fulfilling Isaiah's petition (probably in a much more literal way than even the prophet himself intended or expected): "Oh that you would rend the heavens *and come down*, that the mountains might quake at your presence—as when fire kindles brushwood and the fire causes water to boil—to make your name known to your adversaries, and that the nations might tremble at your presence!" (Isa. 64:1–2, emphasis added). Far from answering in a merely perfunctory and obligatory fashion, God came to our rescue in a manner so outlandish and surprising that no other religion dares claim for their god such a mission. Christianity calls this the mystery of the incarnation, which Paul the apostle describes thusly: "Christ Jesus . . . though he was in the form of God, did not count equality with God a thing to be grasped, but emptied himself, by taking the form of a servant, being born in the likeness of men. And being found in human form, he humbled himself by becoming obedient to the point of death, even death on a cross" (Phil. 2:5–8). We mustn't miss the import of what is being claimed here: God the Son willingly subjected himself not only to the shame of bearing human nature and a human body, but what's more, his humiliation extended as far as Calvary, the hill outside Jerusalem upon which he, though innocent, was crucified after being mocked and beaten by the members of a pagan court.

Scholars of the New Testament puzzle over the Greek term Paul employed in the passage above, which is rendered in English as "Jesus did not count equality with God *a thing to be grasped*." The word appears nowhere else in the New Testament, nor is it found in the Greek translation of the Old. N.T. Wright's best guess is as good as anyone's when he suggests that

---

1. St. Gregory of Nyssa, Orat. catech 15: PG 45, 48B.

the word indicates that Jesus did not consider his equality with God a thing to be *exploited for his own ends*. He writes:

> The real humiliation of the incarnation and the cross is that one who was himself God, and who never during the whole process stopped being God, could embrace such a vocation. The real theological emphasis of the hymn, therefore, is not simply a new view of Jesus. It is a new understanding of God.
>
> The sense of [the Greek] will then be that Christ, in contrast to what one might have expected, refused to take advantage of his position. . . . Nothing described by either [being in the form of God] or [equality with God] is given up; rather, it is reinterpreted, understood in a manner in striking contrast to what one might have expected.[2]

In other words, the very thing that Adam did in the garden—using his privileged status as an excuse to seek to exalt himself beyond what God had commanded—is what Jesus refused to do, despite the temptations of the devil, Peter, and the crowd at the foot of the cross, all of whom suggested he do this very thing.

Why did Jesus resist? When he heard the people cry to him in his period of great agony, "If you are the King of the Jews, save yourself and come down from the cross!" (Luke 22:37; Mark 15:30), why did he choose not to listen? After all, had he not spent his entire earthly life in obedience to his heavenly Father? Had he not denied himself all his days the power, glory, and comfort to which his status as Son of God entitled him? If there was ever a time to invoke his divine rights, was it not when he hung upon the cross, seemingly helpless and consigned to die the death of a common criminal?

Jesus' reason for suffering willingly the shame and death of the cross was that this was how he needed to culminate a life lived thus far in sacrificial, self-giving love to God. Just as Adam was called to offer himself back to God as a sacrifice (metaphorically, and possibly literally as well), so Jesus, as "second Adam," was called to do the same. Only unlike the first Adam, Jesus actually accomplished his mission and the task he was given— he lived a life of humility and sacrifice, and he died a sacrificial death upon the cross for all mankind. Paul tells the Ephesians that "Christ loved us and gave himself up for us, a fragrant offering and sacrifice to God" (5:1), and the writer of Hebrews says, "[Jesus] has appeared once for all at the end of

---

2. Wright, *The Climax of the Covenant*, 83, 84.

the ages to put away sin by the sacrifice of himself" (9:26). We often think of the cross as the moment when Christ laid down his life sacrificially, but that is only partly true. Jesus' entire life, as Wright suggests above, was one of humiliation and sacrifice during which he never once used his divine status of Son of God as something to be exploited for his own ends, his own comfort, or his own will.

Why Sacrifice?

The question may arise, "OK, but *why*? Why did Jesus sacrifice himself? How does that help me today?" It's a good question. After all, many of us who remember our childhood can recall our parents telling us about all the sacrifices they made for our well-being, despite our not being able then to appreciate their relevance to us at the time. Such is often the case with Jesus Christ: we may have grown up hearing all about what he did for us on the cross, all the while scratching our heads and wondering how such a thing is supposed to benefit us today.

The first thing that needs to be established by way of answering this question is the fact that Christ's sacrifice was not offered for his own benefit, but for ours. Jesus, as the divine Son of God, lacked nothing in his relationship to the Father, meaning that his death upon the cross was not intended to benefit himself or add some missing ingredient to his communion with God. The apostle Peter writes, "For Christ also suffered once for sins, the righteous for the unrighteous, *that he might bring us to God*" (I Pet. 3:18, emphasis added). In other words, the intent behind Jesus' self-offering was not to get himself before the Father, but to bring us there.

Why the need for sacrifice to accomplish this, especially the sacrifice of One who was wholly blameless and innocent? The answer, not surprisingly, is found in our previous chapter on sin. Because of our rebellion against God and our breaking of his law, the only means whereby we could stand in his holy presence and be accepted was sacrifice. The great medieval theologian, Anselm, delves deeply into this mystery in his famous work *Cur Deus Homo* (Latin for *Why Did God Become Man*). There Anselm argues that the purpose of Christ's sacrifice was to make *satisfaction* to the Father for sins of men. In order to show that man cannot accomplish this on his own, he writes: "When you render anything to God which you owe him, irrespective of your past sin, you should not reckon this as the debt which you owe for sin . . . . But what do you give to God by your obedience, which is not owed him already, since he demands from you all that you are and have and can become?"³ What Anselm is saying here is that no man can make satisfaction to God for his sin by offering to God what is *already owed* even if no sin were committed. For example, if a son seeks to make amends to his father for denting the family car by promising to always pay for the gas he uses when he drives it, the father would most likely say, "You're supposed to do that anyway! Doing what you're already responsible for doesn't let you off the hook for the further damage you've caused." Likewise we, even if we were able to live lives that were totally pleasing to God, could not thereby make satisfaction to him for our sin, since we ought to be living lives pleasing to him anyway. This, Anselm argues, is why the Son of God needed to assume a human nature and become man: "No man except [Jesus Christ] ever gave to God what he was not obliged to lose, or paid a debt he did not owe. But he freely offered to the Father what there was no need of his ever losing, and paid for sinners what he owed not for himself."⁴ He sums up his argument by saying, "Therefore you make no satisfaction unless you restore something greater than the amount of that obligation" that was due for sin,⁵ moreover that, "[Christ's] life is more lovely than sins are odious,"⁶ and finally, that "the life of [Christ was] so excellent and so glorious as to make ample satisfaction for the sins of the whole world, and infinitely more . . . for he freely gave, for the honor of God, such a gift as surpasses all things else but God himself, and is [therefore] able to atone for all the sins of men."⁷ In other words, Jesus made satisfaction for sinful men by offering to his Father a sacrifice more pleasing than our sins are displeasing.

Union with Christ

Thus far we have seen that Adam's sinful refusal to fulfill the destiny of the species by offering himself back to his Creator as a sacrifice of thanksgiving was atoned for by Jesus, the second Adam, who did what our first father did not. The question now arises, "How do I come to benefit personally from

---

3. Anselm, *Cur Deus Homo*, 226.
4. Ibid., 280.
5. Ibid., 230.
6. Ibid., 263.
7. Ibid., 279.

this sacrifice?" Or to use the phrase that titles this chapter, "How do Jesus and his sacrifice get from eternity to here?"

Much can be said about this issue, but for our purposes here a general answer will have to suffice: *The way we come to benefit from Jesus' sacrifice is by our union with him.* In a mysterious and mystical way, the Christian is united with Christ such that he shares and participates in Jesus' very divine life. In what has been called his "high-priestly prayer," Jesus prays to his Father for his disciples and for those who would believe in him through their testimony:

> "I do not ask for these only, but also for those who will believe in me through their word, that they may all be one, just as you, Father, are in me, and I in you, that they also may be in us, so that the world may believe that you have sent me. The glory that you have given me I have given to them, that they may be one even as we are one, I in them and you in me, that they may become perfectly one, so that the world may know that you sent me and loved them even as you loved me" (John 17:20–23).

Paul the apostle picks up on this idea and furthers it by employing two striking analogies:

> For just as the body is one and has many members, and all the members of the body, though many, are one body, so it is with Christ . . . . We are to grow up in every way into him who is the head, into Christ, from whom the whole body, joined and held together by every joint with which it is equipped, when each part is working properly, makes the body grow so that it builds itself up in love (I Cor. 12:12; Eph. 4:15–16).
>
> Husbands, love your wives, as Christ loved the church and gave himself up for her, that he might sanctify her, having cleansed her by the washing of water with the word, so that he might present the church to himself in splendor, without spot or wrinkle or any such thing, that she might be holy and without blemish. In the same way husbands should love their wives as their own bodies. He who loves his wife loves himself. For no one ever hated his own flesh, but nourishes and cherishes it, just as Christ does the church, because we are members of his body. "Therefore a man shall leave his father and mother and hold fast to his wife, and the two shall become one flesh." This mystery is profound, and I am saying that it refers to Christ and the church (Eph. 5:25–32).

The apostle is saying here that the union the believer has with Christ is similar to the union that the members of a body share with the head, and the union that a husband shares with his wife. In fact, we can go as far as to insist that the illustration actually works in the opposite direction—it's not that our mystical union with Christ is "kind of like" these earthly examples, but that these earthly examples are mere shadowy illustrations of a spiritual union that is much more profound.

It has been suggested that Paul's entire understanding of the Christian life and the centrality of our union with Jesus stemmed from his initial encounter with the risen Lord on the road to Damascus. Before he became a believer, Paul (or Saul, as he was then called) was a zealous opponent and persecutor of Christians, and he was on his way from Jerusalem to Damascus to bind and imprison believers there. While traveling he encountered Christ in a vision, of which we read: "Now as he went on his way, he approached Damascus, and suddenly a light from heaven shone around him. And falling to the ground he heard a voice saying to him, 'Saul, Saul, why are you persecuting me?' And he said, 'Who are you, Lord?' And he said, 'I am Jesus, whom you are persecuting'" (Acts 9:3–5). Don't miss the point that Jesus makes here: so united are Christ and his people that by persecuting the latter, Saul was actually persecuting Jesus himself. Thus it is not a stretch to say that all of Paul's subsequent theological reflection is but an unpacking of this initial idea, that Jesus and his people are one. Further, we could say that if we behold God's entire project of redemption by means of a telescope rather than a microscope, the plan can be understood as a re-creation of man in the image of God, this time grounded in the person and work of the second Adam rather than the first. God is fashioning in Christ a "new man," a mystical body consisting of Jews and Gentiles, people from every kindred, tongue, tribe, and nation, with Christ as the Head of this worldwide, universal, catholic Body (Eph. 2:15; Rev. 5:9). This is what Paul refers to as "the mystery of Christ" and "the mystery of the gospel" (Eph. 3:1–11; 6:19), which is all about unity—God is re-gathering humanity as members of a mystical Body under the authority of a new Head, for the purpose of our fulfilling in Christ the destiny for which we were made in the first place: ". . . making known to us the mystery of his will, according to his purpose, which he set forth in Christ as a plan for the fullness of time, to unite all things in him, things in heaven and things on earth" (Eph. 1:9–10). Therefore Paul can say to the Romans: "I appeal to you therefore, brothers, by the mercies of God, to present your bodies as a living sacrifice, holy and acceptable to God, which is your spiritual worship" (Rom. 12:1). Man's destiny, the very reason for which he was created, is now something that Christ accomplished for us, and further accomplishes in us as we bear our crosses and live a cruciform and sacrificial life.

Before we leave this topic, there is one more question we need to address. If Jesus' sacrifice was for our sake, and if it is by union with him that we come to share in it, how exactly does this work? Mystical union with Christ sounds so ethereal and otherworldly, is it something that we only experience inwardly through navel-gazing and meditation, or does it take some outward and visible form?

What Does Union with Christ Look Like?

The answer to the question posed above is yes, God indeed gives us outward and visible means by which our union with him is established and strengthened. These means are called sacraments, specifically Baptism and Communion (also called the Eucharist or the Lord's Supper). To better explain what the sacraments are, an illustration from the life of Christ may help. In Luke 8:42b-48 we read of Jesus ministering to multitudes of people, and the crowd was pressing in on him from every side. There was a woman in the crowd who had been suffering from a certain malady for many years and had gotten no help from the various physicians she had consulted. She convinced herself that if she could but reach out her hand and touch the hem of Christ's garment, she would be healed of her infirmity. When she did so, she was cured, but her actions did not go unnoticed by Christ. In his words, "I perceive that power has gone out from me" (v. 46). In a similar way, the sacraments have been likened to powers that come forth from the Body of Christ, for by them the Holy Spirit works in the church to bring the sacrifice of Jesus to bear upon God's people in ever increasing and powerful ways, causing our union with him to be deepened.

The way this all begins is through Baptism. Paul asks the Romans, "Do you not know that all of us who have been baptized into Christ Jesus were baptized into his death? We were buried therefore with him by baptism into death.... For we have been united with him in a death like his...." (6:3-4a, 5a). Clearly for Paul, Baptism is much more than a bare sign or sentimental religious ritual. In his mind it is nothing less than the means by which we begin to participate in Jesus' sacrifice, and by which that sacrifice is applied to us.

The Destiny of the Species

If Baptism initiates the believer into the sacrificial life of Christ, that life is sustained by regularly receiving the bread and cup of Communion. By this sacrament, believers participate continually in the sacrifice of Christ in a very physical and tangible way. This sacramental sharing in Jesus' sacrifice is what moved Paul to ask: "The cup of blessing that we bless, is it not a participation in the blood of Christ? The bread that we break, is it not a participation in the body of Christ? Because there is one bread, we who are many are one body, for we all partake of the one bread" (I Cor. 10:16–17). To us who do not live in a culture where sacrifices are regularly offered, the image of blood upon altars can sound primitive and barbaric. But in antiquity, sacrifices and offerings were woven into the religious fabric of society. The believers in Corinth (many of whom converted to Christianity from paganism) would have understood perfectly Paul's analogy, while it may leave us with nothing but furrowed brows and confusion. Let's back up, then, and look at the surrounding context. He writes: "Consider the people of Israel: are not those who eat the sacrifices participants in the altar? What do I imply then? That food offered to idols is anything, or that an idol is anything? No, I imply that what pagans sacrifice they offer to demons and not to God. I do not want you to be participants with demons. You cannot drink the cup of the Lord and the cup of demons. You cannot partake of the table of the Lord and the table of demons" (vv. 18–21). What does Paul mean by all this talk of "participating at the table of demons"? The principle that the apostle is working with—which he considers so obvious that he sees no need to argue for it—is that a person becomes united with, and therefore one with, the sacrifice he offers. Therefore the Israelite or the pagan who offers a sacrifice (whether of an animal, or of grain, or of wine) and then partakes of that sacrifice by eating or drinking it, becomes mystically united with the sacrifice, mystically united with the altar on which it is offered, and mystically united with the God or gods to which it is given. And again, this was simply assumed in times past and completely unobjectionable.

Applying this principle to the Lord's Supper, therefore, means that believers in Christ participate in, and thus become mystically united with, Jesus' sacrifice as they eat the bread and drink the cup, which sacramentally become his very body and blood. As Jesus himself says, "I am the living bread which comes down from heaven. If anyone eats of this bread he will live forever, and the bread that I will give for the life of the world is my flesh ... for my flesh is true food, and my blood is drink indeed" (John 6:51,

55). Just as any ancient sacrifice was incomplete until it was eaten, but once it was consumed it united the worshiper with the one to whom the sacrifice was made, so the Christian's union with Christ and his sacrificial death become actualized each time he receives the bread and cup of Communion.

Jesus drew this parallel between the sacraments and his own death in an encounter he had with two of his disciples, James and John:

> And James and John, the sons of Zebedee, came up to him and said to him, "Teacher, we want you to do for us whatever we ask of you." And he said to them, "What do you want me to do for you?" And they said to him, "Grant us to sit, one at your right hand and one at your left, in your glory." Jesus said to them, "You do not know what you are asking. *Are you able to drink the cup that I drink, or to be baptized with the baptism with which I am baptized?*" And they said to him, "We are able." And Jesus said to them, "The cup that I drink you will drink, and with the baptism with which I am baptized, you will be baptized, but to sit at my right hand or at my left is not mine to grant, but it is for those for whom it has been prepared."
>
> And when the ten heard it, they began to be indignant at James and John. And Jesus called them to him and said to them, "You know that those who are considered rulers of the Gentiles lord it over them, and their great ones exercise authority over them. But it shall not be so among you. But whoever would be great among you must be your servant, and whoever would be first among you must be slave of all. For even the Son of Man came not to be served but to serve, and to give his life as a ransom for many" (Mark 10:35–45, emphasis added).

What these two over-zealous disciples failed to understand was that in Jesus' kingdom greatness comes through sacrifice, and exaltation comes by being lifted up on a cross. But for our purposes here we must note that the images Jesus used to speak about his pending death (and their eventual martyrdom) were "drinking the cup" and "being baptized." Make no mistake, the sacraments are indeed deadly, for they are the concrete means by which we participate in the sacrifice of Christ, and yet are ironically the channels through which the destiny of the species is fulfilled in us.

8

The World's Unworthiness

Mere Mortality

ONE OF THE RIDDLES that philosophers and theologians love to ponder is the question, "Could Jesus have given in to the temptations of the devil and sinned?" Regardless of one's initial response, we must admit that it's a real conundrum: if we say that Jesus could have sinned, then would that mean he would cease to be divine? And is that even possible? But on the other hand if we insist that he could not have sinned, does this mean that the temptations weren't real, or really tempting, at all? I remember thinking about this question several years ago and coming across what I think must be the most clever philosophical solution of all to this riddle (though I won't vouch for its orthodoxy, only for its originality). The philosopher in question insisted that Jesus could not have sinned, *but he didn't know it!* Just as during his earthly ministry Jesus highlighted other things that he did not know (such as the time of his second coming), the same was true here: the Lord's own inability to sin was one of those things that he, while in the flesh, limited himself from knowing. The man propounding this theory then gave an illustration, saying, "If you were to kidnap Clark Kent and hypnotize him so that he doesn't know that he is Superman, and then dangle him off the side of a bridge, would he be scared? Of course he would, despite the fact that if you were to drop him he would fly."

Now, the theory and its illustration may be silly, but they do bring up an interesting point about one's own self-awareness and the behavior that

The World's Unworthiness

should accompany it. If Clark Kent were in his right mind, he would never break a sweat in such a situation since he would know that, if dropped, he could simply fly to safety. In fact, the fear he would display if hypnotized is actually beneath him and unbecoming of one with such super powers, and if he were given a vision of how his hypnotized self would react to that danger, he would probably be embarrassed to see himself carrying on like a mere mortal.

Oddly enough, the apostle Paul rebukes the believers in Corinth for a similar transgression. At the time of his first letter to the church, there were strife and division among the Corinthians, with parties arising within the congregation that were associated with whichever spiritual leaders the believers most identified with. Some were saying, "I am a disciple of Paul," while others boasted, "Well *I* am a disciple of Peter." By way of rebuke for their immaturity, Paul wrote: "And I, brethren, could not speak to you as to spiritual people but as to carnal, as to babes in Christ. I fed you with milk and not with solid food; for until now you were not able to receive it, and even now you are still not able; for you are still carnal. For where there are envy, strife, and divisions among you, are you not carnal and *behaving like mere men*?" (I Cor. 3:1–3, NKJV, emphasis added). When the apostle refers to the Corinthians as "carnal," he means that they are displaying an earthly-mindedness that, while expected among those whose sights are set on the things of this world only, should have no place in the lives of those whose hope lies beyond this present age. But the real zinger, the real insult with which Paul sought to shame his readers, comes at the end of the passage. "When you display such pettiness and division," he asks, "are you not behaving like mere men?" Make no mistake, that was intended to sting! The believers in Corinth, having embraced the destiny of the species by identifying themselves with Christ and his cross and resurrection, have no business behaving like mere earthlings. The citizens of this age and devotees of the here and now have no other choice but to live lives shackled to the whims of this world, for after all, that's who they are. But not the Christian. "Such *were* some of you," says Paul, but no longer: "You were washed, you were sanctified, you were justified in the name of Jesus Christ and by the Spirit of our God" (I Cor. 6:11).

In the sermon on the mount, Jesus has something similar to say to his disciples:

> "You have heard that it was said, 'You shall love your neighbor and hate your enemy.' But I say to you, Love your enemies and pray for

> those who persecute you, so that you may be sons of your Father who is in heaven. For he makes his sun rise on the evil and on the good, and sends rain on the just and on the unjust. For if you love those who love you, what reward do you have? *Do not even the tax collectors do the same*? And if you greet only your brothers, *what more are you doing than others*? Do not even the Gentiles do the same? You therefore must be perfect, as your heavenly Father is perfect" (Matt. 5:43–48, emphasis added).

Don't miss the subtle expectation on Jesus' part for his followers: they were supposed to be different from the worldlings around them. "So you love those who love you?" Jesus says in effect, "Congratulations, you're exactly like everyone else. You're not even rising above the so-called morality of those shady tax collectors! If you are truly a subject of my eternal kingdom, then your life should outshine, and your love for others should transcend, anything we find among the citizens of earth."

Perhaps my favorite biblical passage highlighting the relationship of the citizen of heaven with this present age is found in a seemingly off-handed aside in Hebrews 11, smack dab in the middle of the "hall of faith," the writer's description of the heavenly hope that the saints of old cherished in their hearts. See if you can find it:

> And what more shall I say? For time would fail me to tell of Gideon, Barak, Samson, Jephthah, of David and Samuel and the prophets—who through faith conquered kingdoms, enforced justice, obtained promises, stopped the mouths of lions, quenched the power of fire, escaped the edge of the sword, were made strong out of weakness, became mighty in war, put foreign armies to flight. Women received back their dead by resurrection. Some were tortured, refusing to accept release, so that they might rise again to a better life. Others suffered mocking and flogging, and even chains and imprisonment. They were stoned, they were sawn in two, they were killed with the sword. They went about in skins of sheep and goats, destitute, afflicted, mistreated—of whom the world was not worthy—wandering about in deserts and mountains, and in dens and caves of the earth (vv. 32–38).

Did you catch that? The reason these Old Testament characters were able to display such faith and fortitude in the midst of their torturous afflictions was because they esteemed the world unworthy of them, and its promises and pleasures beneath them. Indeed, the very best, or very worst, that earth has to offer are but petty trifles when considered in the light of the heavenly inheritance that awaits us. Paul certainly thought so, and said as much to the Romans: "For I consider that the sufferings of this present time are not worth comparing with the glory that is to be revealed to us" (Rom. 8:18). What a remarkable statement! If you know anything of the life of Paul, you will know that his sufferings were much greater than what passes for suffering in the American church today (for some reason we seem to think that not getting everything we want in the culture war is tantamount to persecution). Paul described his own afflictions thusly:

> . . . far greater labors, far more imprisonments, with countless beatings, and often near death. Five times I received at the hands of the Jews the forty lashes less one. Three times I was beaten with rods. Once I was stoned. Three times I was shipwrecked; a night and a day I was adrift at sea; on frequent journeys, in danger from rivers, danger from robbers, danger from my own people, danger from Gentiles, danger in the city, danger in the wilderness, danger at sea, danger from false brothers; in toil and hardship, through many a sleepless night, in hunger and thirst, often without food, in cold and exposure. And, apart from other things, there is the daily pressure on me of my anxiety for all the churches (II Cor. 11:23–28).

And yet despite all of this, the apostle deemed his trials, when compared with the glory that awaited him, as unworthy of mention. He uses even stronger language elsewhere:

> But whatever gain I had, I counted as loss for the sake of Christ. Indeed, I count everything as loss because of the surpassing worth of knowing Christ Jesus my Lord. For his sake I have suffered the loss of all things and count them as rubbish, in order that I may gain Christ and be found in him, not having a righteousness of my own that comes from the law, but that which comes through faith in Christ, the righteousness from God that depends on faith—that I may know him and the power of his resurrection, and may share his sufferings, becoming like him in his death, that by any means possible I may attain the resurrection from the dead (Phil. 3:7–11).

Here Paul's point is the same as in Romans 8:18 mentioned above, but only now he shifts gears and applies it in the opposite direction. Not only are his *afflictions* unworthy of comparing with the eternal blessings he waits for, but so are his *accomplishments* (and if you read vv. 5–6 of Philippians 3, you will see that his accomplishments before his conversion to Christianity were very great). Neither Paul's earthly sufferings nor successes were significant enough to draw his attention away from his heavenly citizenship and the eternal reward that awaited him. Of "gaining Christ" and being "found in him," C.S. Lewis writes: "Most certainly, beyond all worlds, unconditioned and unimaginable, transcending discursive thought, there yawns forever the ultimate Fact, the fountain of all other facthood, the burning and undimensioned depth of the Divine Life. Most certainly also, to be united with that Life in the eternal Sonship of Christ is, strictly speaking, *the only thing worth a moment's consideration.*"[1] It is because he lived with his eye on the prize that Paul could say at the end of his life: "For I am already being poured out as a drink offering, and the time of my departure has come. I have fought the good fight, I have finished the race, I have kept the faith. Henceforth there is laid up for me the crown of righteousness, which the Lord, the righteous judge, will award to me on that Day, and not only to me but also to all who have loved his appearing" (II Tim. 4:6–8).

Our Spiritual Engagement Ring

If it is true that mankind has an eternal destiny to which we are all ordered, and for which we are all hardwired, then as I have tried to show, the pleasures and treasures of earth are unworthy of compare with our heavenly inheritance, such that focusing on, pining after, or pursuing the spoils of this age is beneath us. How, then, can we be expected to give expression to such an ideal? If earth and its goods are visible while eternal things remain unseen, then is it not an unreasonable expectation on God's part that we focus on the latter rather than the former?

By way of trying to answer this objection, we must first recognize that the claim that God is unreasonable is itself an oxymoron (sort of like "an unbiased opinion" or "military intelligence"). God is the foundation and source of reason, meaning that when his demands appear unreasonable it is we, and never he, who must examine ourselves and adapt if necessary. But despite the fact that God could, if he so chose, simply demand that we be heavenly- rather than earthly-minded, full stop, the fact is that he recognizes our weakness and has provided for us help toward that end. Or rather, he has provided for us a Helper. On the eve of his betrayal and arrest, Jesus assured the distraught disciples, "I will ask the Father, and he will give you another Helper, to be with you forever, even the Spirit of truth, whom the world cannot receive, because it neither sees him nor knows him. You know

---

1. Lewis, *Miracles*, quoted in *The Quotable Lewis*, 288.

The World's Unworthiness

him, for he dwells with you and will be in you" (John 14:16-17). The gift of the Holy Spirit to indwell God's people was secured by Jesus through his death and resurrection, and was poured out upon the disciples on the Day of Pentecost in Acts 2. It was to this outpouring that Jesus referred in John 7: "On the last day of the feast, the great day, Jesus stood up and cried out, 'If anyone thirsts, let him come to me and drink. Whoever believes in me, as the Scripture has said, "Out of his heart will flow rivers of living water."' Now this he said about the Spirit, whom those who believed in him were to receive, for as yet the Spirit had not been given, because Jesus was not yet glorified" (vv. 37-39). In fact, so important is the Holy Spirit to God's work of redemption that Jesus could actually tell his disciples that it was to their advantage that he leave them and return to his Father in heaven, for unless he left, the Spirit could not come (John 16:7).

What is the connection here between the gift of the Spirit on the one hand, and our ability to live lives that give heed to the destiny of the species on the other? The answer is found in one of the most profound and provocative images that Paul uses to speak of the ministry of the Holy Spirit. He writes:

> For we know that if the tent that is our earthly home is destroyed, we have a building from God, a house not made with hands, eternal in the heavens. For in this tent we groan, longing to put on our heavenly dwelling, if indeed by putting it on we may not be found naked. For while we are still in this tent, we groan, being burdened—not that we would be unclothed, but that we would be further clothed, so that what is mortal may be swallowed up by life. He who has prepared us for this very thing is God, who has given us the Spirit as a guarantee (II Cor. 5:1-5).

As you can see, the context of this passage is the believer's desire to "put off" his earthly body and be "clothed" with his heavenly one. Not only our physical bodies, but the entire physical world, has been subjected to God's curse due to Adam's sin. For this reason, Paul says, "we groan, being burdened." Something in us knows, whether we're believers or not, that things are not as they should be, and that there's something more to life than what we can see all around us.

Here's where the Holy Spirit comes in. Paul says that this longing ache that we experience is there by design, for it is God who has prepared us for this "something more" that we so desire. The apostle then says that God, to help quench this thirst for eternal things, has "given us the Spirit as a guarantee." How, we may ask, does the Holy Spirit serve as a guarantee of our eternal inheritance? The key to answering this question comes from understanding the word that Paul uses for "guarantee." The term comes from the Greek word that denotes the initial giving of funds to insure that one will eventually take full possession of an item he has purchased. In other words, a "down payment" (in fact, in modern Greek the term Paul used literally means "engagement ring"). The gift of the Spirit, in other words, is God's way of assuring us that he will one day possess fully those whom he has redeemed with the blood of Christ, but who have yet to experience that redemption in its totality due to their still being in their earthly bodies, and still living in this present age. Thus the Holy Spirit is our down payment of future glory, our engagement ring who assures us that our heavenly Bridegroom, Jesus Christ, will one day consummate the union that we now experience only in part.

Being Who We Are

How does being sealed with the Spirit and having him dwell in us as a down payment of our future inheritance affect us in the here and now? What exactly does it look like when the theological rubber meets the practical road? Paul, in one of his most profound statements in all his writings, ties together with beautiful clarity our heavenly identity and our earthly conduct:

> If then you have been raised with Christ, seek the things that are above, where Christ is, seated at the right hand of God. Set your minds on things that are above, not on things that are on earth. For you have died, and your life is hidden with Christ in God. When Christ who is your life appears, then you also will appear with him in glory.
>
> Put to death therefore what is earthly in you: sexual immorality, impurity, passion, evil desire, and covetousness, which is idolatry. On account of these the wrath of God is coming. In these you too once walked, when you were living in them. But now you must put them all away: anger, wrath, malice, slander, and obscene talk from your mouth. Do not lie to one another, seeing that you have put off the old self with its practices and have put on the new self, which is being renewed in knowledge after the image of its creator (Col. 3:1–10).

The apostle here insists that if the destiny of the species is indeed something we have come to embrace, then we must behold ourselves

The World's Unworthiness

through eyes of faith. This entails seeing ourselves as God sees us: as raised up with Jesus and enthroned with him in heaven (despite the fact that our physical eyes do not see ourselves in this way yet). Paul further instructs us to seek and set our mind on eternal things, not on earthly ones. This echoes Jesus' own command that we "store up our treasure in heaven, where neither moth nor rust destroys, and where thieves do not break in and steal" (Matt. 6:20), as well as Peter's description of what awaits us as "an inheritance that is imperishable, undefiled, and unfading, kept in heaven for you" (I Pet. 1:4).

While many today would consider these things to be too lofty, ethereal, or pie-in-the-sky to be of any practical use, Paul would strongly disagree. In fact, it is in such otherworldly concepts that he roots his practical, day-to-day instruction. In the passage from Colossians just cited, he moves straight from his consideration of our heavenly identity and inheritance to his prohibition of things like sexual immorality, covetousness, and idolatry. This progression from who we are to what we do flies in the face of the way we often think about God's ethical instruction. Many today see the Bible's prohibitions ("Do not steal," "Do not commit adultery," etc.) as purely negative: "God doesn't want you to be bad, stealing is bad, therefore you shouldn't steal." But such an approach to the Christian life is incredibly shallow and distortive of the gospel, as if God's entire project of redemption can be reduced to mere behavior modification. But on the contrary, every single one of God's positive commands or negative prohibitions is rooted in an identity and heritage we have received from Jesus that, if their full extent and glory were to be revealed to us now, would leave us utterly speechless and faint from shock, anticipation, and probably a little fear as well. The apostle John hints a bit at what lies in store for us when he writes: "Beloved, we are God's children now, and what we will be has not yet appeared; but we know that when he appears we shall be like him, because we shall see him as he is" (I John 3:2). Did you catch that? John says that we do not yet know exactly "what we will be," what our resurrected new bodies will be like. But, he says, we do know this much: we will be like Jesus. C.S. Lewis went so far as to suggest that if we could see one another in our glorified state as we will one day appear, we would be tempted either to fall down in worship or to recoil in fear:

> It is a serious thing to live in a society of possible gods and goddesses, to remember that the dullest most uninteresting person you talk to may one day be a creature which if you saw it now,

you would be strongly tempted to worship, or else a horror and a corruption such as you now meet, if at all, only in a nightmare. All day long we are, in some degree, helping each other to one or the other of these destinations. It is in the light of these overwhelming possibilities, it is with the awe and the circumspection proper to them, that we should conduct all of our dealings with one another, all friendships, all loves, all play, all politics. There are no ordinary people. You have never talked to a mere mortal. Nations, cultures, arts, civilizations—these are mortal, and their life is to ours as the life of a gnat. But it is immortals whom we joke with, work with, marry, snub, and exploit—immortal horrors or everlasting splendors.[2]

As we will discuss eventually, by his resurrection from the dead, our Lord became the firstfruits of a future harvest, and the heavenly glory that he now experiences will one day be fully ours as well. Is it any surprise that John, in the very next verse, says, "And everyone who thus hopes in him purifies himself as he is pure"? Like Paul in Colossians 3, John sees the Christian's purity not in purely negative terms, as if by our sanctity we somehow qualify ourselves to become the heirs of God's eternal inheritance. No, salvation is all of grace, and it is God, and not we ourselves, who qualifies us for his blessings: "May you be strengthened with all power, according to his glorious might, for all endurance and patience with joy, giving thanks to the Father, *who has qualified you to share in the inheritance of the saints in light.* He has delivered us from the domain of darkness and transferred us to the kingdom of his beloved Son, in whom we have redemption, the forgiveness of sins" (Col. 1:11–14, emphasis added). Thus it is our present possession, by virtue of the indwelling Spirit of the risen Christ, of our confident hope that we will one day be like Jesus that causes us to want to be like him *even now*, and "purify ourselves even as he is pure."

Keeping Earth Where It Belongs

My aim is setting these things forth is not to convince you that since heaven is our goal that earth is therefore pointless, bad, or a complete waste of time. On the contrary, earthly pursuits such as work, family, art, sports, and friendship all have the potential to be great blessings in our lives. But (and here's the kicker) this is only possible when we keep earth where it

2. Lewis, *The Weight of Glory*, quoted in Shea, *Mary, Mother of the Son II*, 178.

belongs in our affections, and refuse to let it creep higher than it ought. For the good and worthwhile pursuits of this life, when allowed to eclipse our pursuit of the next, can cease to be blessings and become a curse. The gospel of Luke gives us a perfect example of what happens when one's earthly treasure usurps that of heaven:

> And a ruler asked [Jesus], "Good Teacher, what must I do to inherit eternal life?" And Jesus said to him, "Why do you call me good? No one is good except God alone. You know the commandments: 'Do not commit adultery, Do not murder, Do not steal, Do not bear false witness, Honor your father and mother.'" And he said, "All these I have kept from my youth." When Jesus heard this, he said to him, "One thing you still lack. Sell all that you have and distribute to the poor, and you will have treasure in heaven; and come, follow me." But when he heard these things, he became very sad, for he was extremely rich.
>
> Jesus, seeing that he had become sad, said, "How difficult it is for those who have wealth to enter the kingdom of God! For it is easier for a camel to go through the eye of a needle than for a rich person to enter the kingdom of God." Those who heard it said, "Then who can be saved?" But he said, "What is impossible with man is possible with God."
>
> And Peter said, "See, we have left our homes and followed you." And he said to them, "Truly, I say to you, there is no one who has left house or wife or brothers or parents or children, for the sake of the kingdom of God, who will not receive many times more in this time, and in the age to come eternal life" (18:18–30).

Now, it would be easy to read this account and conclude that Jesus' point was that riches are bad and must be forsaken if one wants to enter heaven, but such a reading would be an oversimplification. For example, if riches *per se* are evil and disqualifying for salvation, then wouldn't my giving them away to another be unloving, since that person would then be scratched off St. Peter's list and turned away at the Pearly Gates because he died with too much money in the bank? No, Jesus' point is not that wealth is wicked, but that an undue attachment to it is. The young man in Luke's account was told to sell his possessions and distribute the proceeds to the poor because, as the unfolding story makes clear, he was more in love with his money than he was with Christ, which is why he left Jesus and walked away sorrowful rather than surrendering his idol and placing God first in his heart.

The Destiny of the Species

The book of Proverbs tells us that "riches do not profit in the day of wrath, but righteousness delivers from death" (11:4). Can you imagine the shame that the rich young ruler will feel on the day of judgment (if indeed he lived out the rest of his earthly life in love with his wealth) upon seeing the glorified Jesus whom his petty earthly treasure forced him to reject? Much like the rich fool in one of Jesus' parables who decided to build bigger barns in which to store his growing possessions only to die that very night and find his heavenly account completely empty, so the young ruler who chose the temporal over the eternal will realize at the final judgment that dying with the most toys wins you nothing, and that the supposedly precious gold that stood between him and Christ is so ordinary and common in heaven that the streets are paved with the stuff.

Tying all of this together, the person who has recognized the destiny of the species and has embraced that destiny for himself should prize heavenly things so highly that the stuff of earth becomes unworthy of compare, unworthy of mention, and unworthy of sharing a place alongside the eternal treasure that awaits him.

9

Divine Conflict Resolution

The Sucker-Punch of Evil

From the years 2001 to 2010, one of my favorite programs on TV was *24*. It starred Keifer Sutherland as special agent Jack Bauer, a member of Los Angeles's Counter Terrorism Unit. As an agent of CTU, Bauer's entire life was dedicated to fighting the most dangerous and sociopathic terrorists imaginable, often at the expense of his relationship with his own wife and daughter. Early in the first season Bauer's daughter is abducted, a trial that has the effect of bringing him closer to his increasingly estranged wife, Teri, and helping restore their fractured relationship as they desperately try to bring her back to safety. As the season progresses we begin to see the trust between Jack and Teri rebuilt, and when their daughter is rescued and the larger crisis averted, things look as though there will be a true feel-good, storybook ending: the threat was quelled, Jack's family was safe, and his marriage was on the way to being fully restored. *Not so fast.* In what could only be described as a serious sucker-punch, roughly ten minutes before the first season's conclusion, Jack's wife Teri is taken hostage by a traitorous double-agent within CTU before the agent escapes and eludes capture. When Jack finally discovers Teri, he finds her tied to a chair, slumped over, dead from a gunshot to the stomach. The screen then goes to black, and *24* season 1 comes to an end.

A few observations: first, I refuse to take responsibility for any spoilers in the above paragraph. This stuff aired more than a decade ago, so if you're just finding out about it now it's your own fault. Secondly, the killing of Teri Bauer—a character so central to the program—demonstrated a real gutsiness on the part of the show's producers that made the audience realize that anything could happen on *24*, no matter how shocking or cruel. And thirdly, in this case life often mirrors art, and therefore one of the most profound and troubling mysteries we encounter is the one about bad things happening to good people.

"Maybe Your Hands Aren't Free?"

The great medieval philosopher Thomas Aquinas reportedly once admitted that though there are plenty of arguments against the existence of God, there is only one good one: the argument from the problem of evil. The argument has been framed in various ways, but one of the simplest is like this: If God were good, he would want to put an end to evil; if God were all powerful, he would be able to put an end to evil; but evil exists; therefore God is either not good, not all powerful, or he doesn't exist at all.

I don't think it would be too much of a stretch to suggest that of all the places where the problem of evil is most wrestled with and discussed, it is in the realm of art, and more specifically, popular music, where the theme is most prominent. Indeed, we could almost insist that without a profound recognition of evil on the part of musicians and songwriters, there would be no popular music at all. Consider The Beatles' song "Yesterday" when, Paul McCartney sings, "all my troubles seemed so far away, but now it looks as though they're here to stay," which leads him to lament, "How I long for yesterday."[1] In one of my favorite songs by Led Zeppelin, Robert Plant sings about the pursuit of innocence and love after being ill-treated by "a woman unkind": "I made up my mind, going to make a new start; I'm going to California with an aching in my heart." When he gets there, he finds only more disillusionment and abuse:

> *It seems that the wrath of the gods*
> *Got a punch on the nose, and it started to flow;*
> *I think I might be sinking.*
> *Throw me a line, if I reach it in time*
> *I'll meet you up there where the path*
> *Runs straight and high.*

---

1. The Beatles, "Yesterday" from *Help!* (1965).

By the song's end, all the protagonist can do is spend his time "telling myself it's not as hard, hard, hard as it seems."[2] One of the most honest and poignant expressions of lamentation toward God and his seeming inactivity and unwillingness to deal with the evil that besets the citizens of this world comes from the song with which U2 concluded their album, *Pop*:

> *Jesus, Jesus help me;*
> *I'm alone in this world,*
> *And a fucked up world it is, too.*
>
> *Tell me, tell me the story,*
> *The one about eternity,*
> *And the way it's all gonna be.*
>
> *Jesus, I'm waiting here, Boss;*
> *I know you're looking out for us,*
> *But maybe your hands aren't free.*
>
> *Your Father, He made the world in seven,*
> *He's in charge of Heaven,*
> *Will you put a word in for me?*

The chorus that follows these accusations is the simple plea, "Wake up. Wake up, dead Man."[3] Indeed, so seemingly hopeless is man's plight that Conor Oberst can ask the chilling question, "If I sold my soul for a bag of gold, which one of us would be the fool?"[4] An entire volume could be written tracing in popular music this theme of man's being confronted with, and confounded by, the effects of evil in the world (just listen to The Smiths or Radiohead if you don't believe me).

What is true of music can also be said of the majority of the twentieth-century American writers and poets to whom I am drawn. Without profound evil, what would Flannery O'Connor have had to talk about? Would Truman Capote's best work have been written? Would the poetry and prose of Bukowski have been necessary? "Art that doesn't bear witness to the opaque, the mysterious, or even allow any ambiguity is propaganda at best and, at worst, a ministry of death, an exercise in sentimentalizing, self-congratulatory delusion. . . . Every expression of 'this isn't the way it has to be' and every call for resistance, however modest, is a step in the direction

2. Led Zeppelin, "Going to California" from *Led Zeppelin IV* (1971).
3. U2, "Wake Up Dead Man" from *Pop* (1997).
4. Bright Eyes, "Don't Know When, But a Day is Gonna Come" from *Lifted, or The Story Is in the Soil, Keep Your Ear to the Ground* (2002).

The Destiny of the Species

of life. Only the clear gaze and the honest word can move us to wonder how one might best remain in light or what little of it can still be discerned in the gathering dark."[5] In a word, no amount of theoretical relativism can ever soothe the soul of the sufferer, and academic opinions about there being "no black or white but only different shades of gray" cannot come to the rescue of the one staring down the barrel of a gun. The problem of evil is real, and to deny it is to call one's own humanity itself into question.

My aim in this chapter is to address the issue of evil, but not so much from a philosophical perspective as from an eschatological one. The Greek word *eschatos* means "last," and it often refers to man's final end. The approach I want to take to the problem of evil, then, is one that seeks to consider the issue from the standpoint of the story that God is telling, which is far from over.

"Curse God and Die!"

The *locus classicus* of the Bible's treatment of the problem of evil is the book of Job, where "bad things happening to good people" is an understatement. The story opens with an introduction of Job as "blameless and upright, one who feared God, and turned away from evil" (1:1). Job's uprightness results in God boasting about him to the devil in the throne room in heaven, upon which the devil retorts, "Does Job fear God for no reason? Have you not put a hedge around him and his house and all that he has, on every side? You have blessed the work of his hands, and his possessions have increased in the land. But stretch out your hand and touch all that he has, and he will curse you to your face" (1:9–11). In other words, the devil says, Job is only playing a game of *quid pro quo*. If God were to turn off the spigot of material blessings, Job would be whistling a different (and darker) tune in no time. God took Satan up on his challenge and permitted the devil to afflict Job by stripping him of all his earthly comforts, provided Job himself not be touched. Thus through a series of calamities and pestilences, Job lost his donkeys, camels, oxen, sheep, servants, and even his own children.

One can only imagine the pain, confusion, and anger at God Job must have been feeling upon experiencing such horrific loss. This is what makes his response so remarkable: "Naked I came from my mother's womb, and naked shall I return. The Lord gave, and the Lord has taken away; blessed be the name of the Lord" (1:21).

---

5. Dark, *Apocalypse*, 21, 65.

Satan, upon being proven wrong, did not let up, but exclaimed, "Skin for skin! All that a man has he will give for his life. But stretch out your hand and touch his bone and his flesh, and he will curse you to your face" (2:4). God again gave the devil leave to afflict Job, upon the condition that his life be spared. The devil then struck Job with weeping sores from head to foot, to the point where his condition was so loathsome that even his wife said to him, "Do you still hold fast your integrity? Curse God and die!" To this Job replied, "You speak as one of the foolish women would speak. Shall we receive good from God, and shall we not receive evil?" (2:9–10). To his immense credit Job understood that all things come from God's hand, and that if he chooses to curse rather than bless, it is the responsibility of the faithful to trust him and his infinite wisdom even when they do not understand his ways.

At this point the book begins to get especially interesting, as Job receives visits from three of his friends seeking to impart encouragement and advice. Despite having no firsthand evidence, the assumption on the part of Job's friends is that he is obviously hiding some great sin, and if he would just come out and confess it, God would forgive him and restore his health and his fortune. In response to this accusation Job denies any wrongdoing on his own part, calling them "miserable counselors," and goes so far as to insist that if it were possible to find an impartial judge and take God to court, he would win his case!

When Job finally finishes justifying himself and screaming his own innocence in spite of God's cruelty—one commentator joked that the most important line in the entire book is, "The words of Job are ended"—God, with the gentleness but firmness of a Father, explains to Job that he has no idea what he is talking about, and that he would be better off if he just shuts up for a while and lets the Lord talk. God then rebukes Job's three friends for misrepresenting him as though he were angry with Job, commanding them to offer sacrifices so that their folly might be forgiven. Finally, God restores Job's fortunes and blesses him beyond anything he had experienced before. The final verse in the book reads, "And Job died, an old man, and full of days."

You're probably wondering, "What in the world was God doing in the book of Job? How could a good God put a man through all that just to prove a point?" These are important questions and, as I said above, my aim is to address them not as a philosopher but as a character in the divine drama. Don't get me wrong, there are philosophical answers to this puzzle (such as pointing out that the goodness of God is not identical to the goodness of a man, any more than the goodness of a man is identical to the goodness of a dog), but for those of us in the thick of hardship and affliction like Job was, beard-stroking philosophical musings won't cut it. No, God is not merely the Object of man's contemplation, he is the Subject and Playwright in whose story we find ourselves. As one rabbi put it, "God is not nice. God is not an uncle. God is an earthquake."[6] Peter Kreeft writes: "If God himself, the all-wise designer of the whole story we are in, were *not* this shocking and surprising 'Lord of the Absurd' but rational, predictable, comfortable, and convenient, then life would not be a mystery to be lived but a problem to be solved, not a love story but a detective story, not a tragicomedy but a formula. For tragedy and comedy are the two primary forms of mystery, and if Job teaches us anything, it is that we are living in a mystery."[7] Life, in other words, is not so much a question but a quest, which is a question that is lived out, suffered through, endured, pondered, and wrestled with in real-life sweat and toil and anguish and tears. And ironically, there simply is no other path to true happiness.

> Job may be short-range unhappy, but he is long-range happy, even in the sense of satisfaction. Job is satisfied at the end. . . . He is in a drama, a story, after all, and only in the earlier acts, the earlier chapters. How can you understand the point of Act II until you get to Act V? The problem of evil, as lived rather than as thought, is a problem in a story, in time, and Scripture's one-word answer to the problem is "wait."
>
> When Saint Thomas Aquinas stated in the *Summa* the problem of evil as one of the two objections to the existence of God, he remembered what many philosophers forget: that the solution, God's solution, is concrete, not abstract; dramatic, not schematic; an event in time, not a timeless truth.[8]

"God's solution is an event in time." It is to that consideration that we now turn.

---

6. Rabbi Abraham Heschel, cited in Kreeft, *Three Philosophies*, 63.
7. Ibid., 56, emphasis original.
8. Ibid., 75.

The Death of Death

If the issue of human suffering were merely a philosophical problem to be pondered, it could be considered in a classroom; if evil were just a question of misfiring synapses in the brain, it could be resolved in a laboratory; if wickedness were simply an issue of behavior modification, it could be addressed from a therapist's couch. But if our suffering evil without and combatting it within is a result of sin, then it cannot be dealt with in a lecture hall or an ivory tower. This brings us to the "concrete event" alluded to above: evil has indeed been dealt a fatal blow, and it happened on a hill outside Jerusalem, from a wooden cross, by a Man of Sorrows who knew a thing or two about bad things happening to good people. In a word, God has addressed the problem of evil in the most ironic and unexpected way imaginable: by allowing the greatest evil that hell could conjure to be visited upon his own sinless and beloved Son.

Think about it: if Job was righteous, was not Jesus more so? If Job suffered, did not Jesus suffer more? And yet this hellish example of wickedness is the very means by which God solved—and is solving—the problem of evil. To illustrate the seeming incongruity of using *that* means for *this* end, consider a familiar account from the gospels:

> Immediately [Jesus] made the disciples get into the boat and go before him to the other side, while he dismissed the crowds. And after he had dismissed the crowds, he went up on the mountain by himself to pray. When evening came, he was there alone, but the boat by this time was a long way from the land, beaten by the waves, for the wind was against them. And in the fourth watch of the night he came to them, walking on the sea. But when the disciples saw him walking on the sea, they were terrified, and said, "It is a ghost!" and they cried out in fear. But immediately Jesus spoke to them, saying, "Take heart; it is I. Do not be afraid." (Matt. 14:22–27)

This account is familiar to Christians and non-Christians alike, so familiar, in fact, that we can easily miss an obvious detail that sheds great light on the way God often works. What was it that the disciples in the boat were afraid of? The answer is simple: they were afraid of the storm, of the waves, and of water getting into the boat and causing it to sink. But what was the means Jesus used to save the disciples from the object of their fear? He walked to them *on the water*. To put it plainly, Jesus used that which the disciples feared as the means of delivering them from it!

The Destiny of the Species

The same is true in the spiritual realm. Consider what the writer to the Hebrews says: "Since therefore the children [of Abraham] share in flesh and blood, he himself likewise partook of the same things, that *through death he might destroy the one who has the power of death*, that is, the devil, and deliver all those who through fear of death were subject to lifelong slavery" (2:14–15, emphasis added). In the same way that water was the means to deliver the disciples from their fear of the waves, so in the drama of redemption, the means God chooses to free us from our fear of death is death itself. In a shocking display of spiritual judo, God actually beats the devil at his own game by using the force of his power against him. After possessing Judas Iscariot and compelling him to betray the Lord and hand him over to the Jewish authorities (who eventually turned him over to the Romans who actually had the power to condemn Jesus to death), the devil certainly believed he had thwarted God's plan. What he couldn't have anticipated—indeed, what none of us (including the disciples themselves) could have foreseen—was that the very thing that all people, including the pious rabbinical scholars of the day, unanimously considered a curse (namely death) would become the greatest source of blessing for fallen mankind.

A Grand and Glorious Finale

How can such a shameful event be called a blessing? How can good come out of such evil? Surely this is an example of mere euphemism, sort of like calling a used Lexus "pre-owned," right?

Not necessarily. If Jesus' death had been the end of the story, if he had remained in the tomb the way everyone expected him to, then the answer would be *yes*, calling his crucifixion a blessing would be stubborn and pathetic, a bury-our-head-in-the-sand refusal to face the fact that we lost, and that our story is a tragedy that can offer no more help to lost people than *Aesop's Fables* or William Bennett's *Book of Virtues*.

But of course, Jesus did not remain in the tomb, but he rose from the dead on the third day. The resurrection of the Son of God, being perhaps the most miraculous event ever witnessed by mankind, should be one of those things whose significance is easy to estimate. For example, if an alien spaceship touched down to earth at the 50 yard-line during the Super Bowl halftime show in full view of millions of people, would anyone argue that the ramifications of such an event must not be overstated? Of course not! In fact, an occurrence of that magnitude would cause mankind to rethink their entire worldview and begin to consider everything else in the light of such a spectacle. Why, then, do we insist upon treating the resurrection of Christ as though it has little relevance for life's biggest questions, especially the one we are considering in this chapter?

The raising of Jesus from the dead is more than a mere apologetic tactic or a divine "I told you so" delivered to the Lord's opponents, as though its relevance is exhausted once a person relents and admits that Jesus really is who he claims to be. On the contrary, the relevance of the resurrection extends much further than we can estimate, for in it we find the key to unlocking the mystery of the problem of evil. How does the resurrection do that? The answer is that it grants us a glimpse of the final chapter of our earthly story before we actually experience it. To better understand this idea, consider the metaphor Paul employs in his treatment of the resurrection in I Corinthians:

> But in fact Christ has been raised from the dead, the firstfruits of those who have fallen asleep. For as by a man came death, by a man has come also the resurrection of the dead. For as in Adam all die, so also in Christ shall all be made alive. But each in his own order: Christ the firstfruits, then at his coming those who belong to Christ. Then comes the end, when he delivers the kingdom to God the Father after destroying every rule and every authority and power. For he must reign until he has put all his enemies under his feet. The last enemy to be destroyed is death (15:20–26).

Note the term "firstfruits" in the passage above, which occurs twice. It's an odd term for many today (so odd, in fact, that my spell-check underlines it in red). What is the apostle referring to here when he says that the risen Christ is "the firstfruits" of those who have died?

The term is an agricultural one, denoting the initial growth of a crop that is offered to God, thereby sanctifying the entire harvest that follows it. For instance, if a farmer wanted to demonstrate his thankfulness to God for his abundant provision, he couldn't offer the entire harvest to God as a sacrifice since, if he did, he would have nothing left with which he could provide for his own needs. Instead he would offer the firstfruits to God, and those initial fruits would represent the entire crop that was to come.

What, then, is Paul's point in applying this metaphor to Jesus and his resurrection? The apostle likens the people of God to a great harvest of resurrected saints, and the firstfruits of that harvest is Jesus himself, who is the first Person to rise from the dead in a glorified body, as well as the One

The Destiny of the Species

who sanctifies the rest of the crop and ensures their future resurrection on the last Day. This is why Paul says that there is an order to the resurrection: Christ is raised first, and then those who belong to him will be raised when he returns.

How does this apply to the focus of this chapter, the problem of evil? The apostle himself answers this question at the end of I Corinthians 15 where he says:

> Behold! I tell you a mystery. We shall not all sleep, but we shall all be changed, in a moment, in the twinkling of an eye, at the last trumpet. For the trumpet will sound, and the dead will be raised imperishable, and we shall be changed. For this perishable body must put on the imperishable, and this mortal body must put on immortality. When the perishable puts on the imperishable, and the mortal puts on immortality, then shall come to pass the saying that is written:
>
> > *Death is swallowed up in victory.*
> > *O death, where is your victory?*
> > *O death, where is your sting?*
>
> The sting of death is sin, and the power of sin is the law. But thanks be to God, who gives us the victory through our Lord Jesus Christ.
>
> Therefore, my beloved brothers, be steadfast, immovable, always abounding in the work of the Lord, knowing that in the Lord your labor is not in vain (vv. 51–58).

Did you catch that last bit? The Christian's "labor is not in vain," for our union with Christ—the *risen* Christ—means that both our triumphs *and* our trials, our successes *and* our sufferings, all have meaning, and that meaning will one day be made plain, but only in the context of the destiny of the species and the divine drama that God is staging, of which we are now only in the midst.

10

Apocalypse Eventually

Long-Term Order, Short-Term Chaos

IF THERE EVER WERE a metaphor for the chronologically mind-blowing uniqueness of the Christian life, it would have to be Christopher Nolan's 2000 film, *Memento*. Some years prior to the story's beginning, Nolan's protagonist, Leonard Shelby, underwent a significantly traumatic episode in his life that precipitated his suffering from a condition called anterograde amnesia, which impairs his ability to form new memories (meaning that, while he can remember the events leading up to that episode, he forgets everything that happens after it in roughly five minutes). What makes the storytelling so unique is that the film is presented in two distinct sets of short sequences: the first (shot in black and white) moves in chronological order, while the second (shot in color) moves in reverse order, and at the conclusion of the film the two sets of sequences meet. Admittedly, a film like *Memento* takes some getting used to and may in fact require multiple viewings before the viewer truly wraps his mind around what he is watching. But what I find especially instructive and apropos for our purposes about this form of storytelling is the juxtaposition between knowing how the story ends on the one hand, but having next to no idea how it will arrive there on the other.

Such is the Christian life. On one level we know how the story ends, namely, with the destiny of the species being fulfilled perfectly according to God's purpose and plan. How exactly the details will unfold, however, is anyone's guess. Now if you are anything like me, you function better within a given moment if you know how that moment fits in with the overall schedule for the day. For example, just a few minutes ago I mapped out my own day's plans, figuring out that if I want to be back home in time to take my son to his karate class at 5:00 I need to leave my previous meeting at 4:30, which means it needs to start by 3:00 (and if I want to work out and shower beforehand, I need to be home from the gym by 2:00, etc.). This mental scheduling of my afternoon on my part allows me to focus now, at 10:06 in the morning, on working on this book. If I had no idea what the rest of my day would entail, it would make concentrating on anything in the present exceedingly difficult.

But unfortunately for people like me, God simply does not see fit to provide a detailed description of all the steps connecting the present with our ultimate destination, but instead asks us to walk by faith, and not by sight (II Cor. 5:7). Like the viewer of *Memento*, our knowledge of the final outcome doesn't remove the need to pay close attention to all the unexpected details along the way (especially because in the Christian life the details of our present moment play a pretty significant role in how things will play out in the end!). Therefore as we draw our consideration of the destiny of the species to a close, I would like to tie together what we have learned thus far, with a particular focus on the need for patient endurance amid all the details and seeming distractions of this present age.

Of Toothaches, Tribulation, and Apocalyptic Response

In the Bible's final book, Revelation, we find a call issued over and over again to patiently endure through the struggles of life as we keep our eyes fixed upon the heavenly reward that awaits us:

> I, John, your brother and partner in the tribulation and the kingdom and the *patient endurance* that are in Jesus, was on the island called Patmos on account of the word of God and the testimony of Jesus (1:9).

> "I know your works, your toil and your *patient endurance*, and how you cannot bear with those who are evil, but have tested those who call themselves apostles and are not, and found them to be false" (2:2).

> "I know your works, your love and faith and service and *patient endurance*, and that your latter works exceed the first" (2:19)
>
> "Because you have kept my word about *patient endurance*, I will keep you from the hour of trial that is coming on the whole world, to try those who dwell on the earth" (3:10).
>
> If anyone is to be taken captive, to captivity he goes; if anyone is to be slain with the sword, with the sword must he be slain. Here is a call for the *endurance* and faith of the saints (13:10).
>
> And the smoke of their torment goes up forever and ever, and they have no rest, day or night, these worshipers of the beast and its image, and whoever receives the mark of its name. Here is a call for the *endurance* of the saints, those who keep the commandments of God and their faith in Jesus (14:11–12).

The call to endure necessitates that those things which are to be endured are difficult rather than delightful. As I pointed out in my book *Dual Citizens*, one does not "endure" a delicious meal or a fine glass of wine. Rather, endurance applies to things like toothaches, long layovers, and stones in one's shoe. As much as we may wish that the Christian life were like the former examples, it's in fact a lot more like the latter ones. The picture the Bible paints of our pilgrimage to glory is that of a race, a battle, a wrestling match, and a life characterized by constant, daily death to ourselves and our own comfort and plans for our lives.

If you are newer to the Christian faith (or even if you're just a curious onlooker), you may be confused at hearing that the life of a believer is one of struggle rather than success, of trial rather than triumph. This confusion is without doubt due to the popular message of the American gospel which masquerades these days as the real thing, according to which Jesus' whole purpose in coming to earth was to fix our brokenness and heal all of our sad disillusionment. In a word, the gospel has become therapy and Jesus has become a life coach whose purported message differs from Dr. Phil's in ways that are becoming increasingly more difficult to detect.

When the destiny of the species has become neutered to the point of losing any hint of otherworldliness or protest against our earthly status quo, it is no wonder that people become attracted to the watered down version of the gospel, the one that posits "a God without wrath [who] brought men without sin into a kingdom without judgment through a Christ without a

The Destiny of the Species

cross."¹ And furthermore, when "an air-conditioned spirituality that loves gloss over substance" becomes the expected norm, it just gets more and more difficult to "prefer the pounding headache of looking hard at the world over the blissful, happy-ending incomprehensibility of Technicolor."² The proper way to navigate the tragedy and evil that characterize this present age is not to bury one's head in the sand, and neither is it to expect Christ to be a present cure-all or Christianity an earthly panacea. No, an apocalyptic, future-focused, and heavenly-minded posture looks suffering square in the face, but then looks beyond it to what comes next. We don't stop reading in the middle of the story, neither do we expect this wilderness world to be our final destination. David Dark writes:

> If [the powers that be] are the boot that, to borrow Orwell's phrase, presses down upon the human face forever, apocalyptic is the speech of that human face. Apocalyptic denies, in spite of all the appearances to the contrary, the "forever" part. For both the human wielder of the boot and the very human face beneath it, apocalyptic has a way of curing deafness and educating the mind. In our confusion, we're accustomed to according the titles of good news and "a positive message" to the most soul-sucking, sentimental fare imaginable. Any song or story that deals with conflict by way of a strained euphemistic spin, a cliché, or a triumphal cupcake ending strikes us as the best in family entertainment. This is the opposite of apocalyptic. Apocalyptic maximizes the reality of human suffering and folly before daring a word of hope (lest too light winning make the prize light). The hope has nowhere else to happen but the valley of the shadow of death.³

Contrary to what is often taught and exhibited by American believers, the cry of the Christian ought not to be "Peace! Peace!" when there is no peace, nor a sentimental suggestion that "War Is Over! If You Want It," but instead a maximizing of the bad news together with an equally stubborn insistence that the good news outshines it, and that the sufferings of this present time are not worthy of being compared with the glory that shall be revealed to us (Rom. 8:18).

---

1. Niebuhr, *The Kingdom of God in America*, 193.
2. Dark, *Apocalypse*, 79.
3. Ibid., 10.

Sounding the Blue Note

I remember with sincere fondness my early days as a Christian at Calvary Chapel of Costa Mesa in Southern California. One of the things that makes me most nostalgic about that period in my life is the music and praise songs that we would sing—in fact, whenever I hear a snippet of one of those tunes it brings back a flood of good memories of my first days as a believer and the utter newness of my faith. One thing I came to discover later in my Christian life, however, was that there was something of an imbalance when it came to the praise choruses that were played at church. While most of them were adapted straight from the words of Scripture (usually the psalms), they seemed to focus solely on the psalms, or the parts of psalms, that highlighted personal triumph, subjective security, and intimacy with God, while ignoring completely the equally-biblical dynamics of lamentation and struggle. Our praise songs would echo passages like, "As a deer pants for flowing streams, so pants my soul for you, O God" (Psa. 42:1), or, "You are a hiding place for me; you preserve me from trouble; you surround me with shouts of deliverance" (Psa. 32:7), but conspicuous by their absence were any songs that sounded like this:

> I am weary with my moaning;
> every night I flood my bed with tears;
> I drench my couch with my weeping.
> My eye wastes away because of grief;
> it grows weak because of all my foes. (Psa. 6:6–7)

Or this:

> How long, O Lord? Will you forget me forever?
> How long will you hide your face from me?
> How long must I take counsel in my soul
> and have sorrow in my heart all the day?
> How long shall my enemy be exalted over me? (Psa. 13:1–2)

John Calvin claimed that the book of Psalms could be aptly titled "An Anatomy of All the Parts of the Soul," for each and every human emotion is vividly described therein. I would echo him on this point, but be quick to add—for the sake of our modern ears—that the emotions expressed in the Psalms include the bad ones, the embarrassing ones, and the ones we would be ashamed to exhibit at church on a Sunday.

In a written introduction to the Psalter, Bono, lead singer of the band U2, had this to say about his own experience with the Psalms of David:

The Destiny of the Species

> At age 12, I was a fan of David. . . . The words of the psalms were as poetic as they were religious. David was a dramatic character, because before he could fulfill the prophecy and become the king of Israel, he had to take quite a beating. He was forced into exile and ended up in a cave in some no-name border town facing the collapse of his ego and abandonment by God. But this is where the soap opera got interesting, this is where David was said to have composed his first psalm—a blues. That's what a lot of the psalms feel like to me, the blues. Man shouting at God, "My God, my God, why hast thou forsaken me?" Abandonment, displacement, this is the stuff of my favorite psalms. The Psalter may be a font of gospel music, but for me it's in his despair that the psalmist really reveals the nature of his special relationship with God. Honesty, even to the point of anger. "How long, Lord? Wilt thou hide thyself forever?" as in Psalm 89, or "Answer me when I call" in Psalm 5. . . . I had thought of [the cry "How long?"] as a nagging question—pulling at the hem of an invisible deity whose presence we glimpse only when we act in love. How long . . . hunger? How long . . . hatred? How long until creation grows up from the chaos of its precociousness, until hell-bent adolescence has been discarded? I thought it odd that the vocalizing of such questions could bring me so much comfort.[4]

Many today might also find it odd that anyone could find "comfort" in a biblical writer's expressions of frustration with God's seeming abandonment of him, but for my part, I relate to Bono's sentiments perfectly. Perhaps it's the cynical Gen-Xer in me that finds the saccharine-infused, syrupy, sugar-coated message of so-called Christianity, according to which we are to expect lives of uninterrupted goose-bumps and bliss, to be so inauthentic and patronizing that it ends up doing more harm than good (not to mention the fact that anyone who's paying even the smallest amount of attention to the real world can see right through this façade).

"But," you may object, "isn't all this focus on difficulty and endurance just depressing? Isn't the job of Christianity to make people feel better, rather than worse?" Before we answer that question, we must first admit that there is more than one way to make a person feel good: we can do it by telling him the truth, but we can also do it by lying to him (and often it is the second option that's easiest). For example, back in the garden of Eden it was the devil, and not God, who delivered to man a message of ease and triumph:

4. *The Book of Psalms*, vi—xi.

> Now the serpent was more crafty than any other beast of the field that the Lord God had made. He said to the woman, "Did God actually say, 'You shall not eat of any tree in the garden'?" And the woman said to the serpent, "We may eat of the fruit of the trees in the garden, but God said, 'You shall not eat of the fruit of the tree that is in the midst of the garden, neither shall you touch it, lest you die.'" But the serpent said to the woman, "You will not surely die. For God knows that when you eat of it your eyes will be opened, and you will be like God, knowing good and evil." So when the woman saw that the tree was good for food, and that it was a delight to the eyes, and that the tree was to be desired to make one wise, she took of its fruit and ate, and she also gave some to her husband who was with her, and he ate (Gen. 3:1–6).

Satan was, in effect, urging man to buck against his proper station—that of a creature—and yearn for a degree of glory that was outside his grasp. While Adam would have indeed graduated to greater glory eventually, the devil was tempting him to stretch forth his hand and seize what was not yet his to enjoy. My point here is not to retread material already covered, but rather to point out that the devil's temptation of Adam fulfilled, rather ironically, the requirements for a good Christian message for many today, namely, it was a message that made Adam feel good because it filled his head with big ideas about avoiding suffering and getting what he wanted as quickly and painlessly as possible. But such a message, despite its short-term comfort, is a lie. And likewise, any sermon, praise song, or Christian book that promises a life devoid of difficulty is deceptive at best, and devilish at worst.

It requires faith, and guts, and a lot of trust in God to truly reckon with our earthly lot this side of heaven. Any preaching, teaching, or ministry in general, in order to qualify as Christian, must tell us the truth about what we are to expect in this present evil age. "Apocalyptic expression," writes Dark, "tells us what we're trying with all our might to forget. It shows us the multifaceted ways in which we've become morally bankrupt and emotionally numb. We've fallen a considerable distance when we can only recognize such work as depressing. What could be more depressing than entertainment that serves as a kind of soul anesthetic, broken cisterns that will hold no water, sentimental bubbles that distract us long enough to make us forget whatever it was that had us wondering (for one saving moment) what was wrong."[5] If Dark is correct about soul-anesthetizing art being a distracting

---

5. Dark, Apocalypse, 72.

and sentimental bubble that can hold no true content, how much more tragic is it when it's not entertainment but Christian ministry that falls prey to such a description? There's simply no way around it, the Christian life is one of struggle and endurance, with the goal that we may be able to echo Paul's words, written toward the end of his own life: "For I am already being poured out as a drink offering, and the time of my departure has come. I have fought the good fight, I have finished the race, I have kept the faith. Henceforth there is laid up for me the crown of righteousness, which the Lord, the righteous judge, will award to me on that Day, and not only to me but also to all who have loved his appearing" (II Tim. 4:6–8).

The Key to Feeling Homesick at Home

As we bring our consideration to a close, I would reiterate what I said way back at the beginning of this book, namely, that Darwin's account of the origin of our species—particularly when pursued to the point of eliminating the supernatural altogether—simply fails to scratch our collective itch or meet us where we truly are. It is not the Darwinian notion of mere biology or even the biblical idea of sinfulness that captures our identity and defines us. What needs to be said loud and clear, writes Mark Shea, is that

> . . . we are made in the image of God and that our fallenness, though very real, does not name or define us: only Jesus Christ does. Though sin has defaced the image of God in countless ways, it nonetheless is false to say that we are essentially made of the chaos and dehumanization of sin. We are not mere animals, statistical averages, cogs in a machine, sophisticated primordial ooze, or a jangling set of complexes, appetites, tribal totems, Aryan supermen, or totally depraved Mr. Hydes. We are made by God, for God, and redeemed by God, for God. God has, in fact, joined himself irrevocably to our human nature and raised it up to dwell in the heavenlies with him in the Person of Christ Jesus. Because of this overwhelming victory over sin, Jesus, not fallen Adam, is the deepest truth about who man is.
>
> All the philosophies of pride, which love diagrams more than faces, see human beings as means to ends, not as the only creatures that God willed into existence out of love. It matters little what the end is if the end is not God and our eternal union with him. Whether it's a sustainable green economy, the glory of

world socialism, a race of thoroughbreds, or the American Way, the inherent claim of all ideology is that persons matter less than systems.[6]

Indeed, no theory about where we come from is complete until it addresses where we're going, for the mystery of human existence can never be solved unless we consider that our lives, far from being a purposeless cosmic accident, are in fact intended *for* something, and something very specific. C.S. Lewis writes:

> The mold in which a key is made would be a strange thing, if you had never seen a key: and the key itself a strange thing if you had never seen a lock. Your soul has a curious shape because it is a hollow made to fit a particular swelling in the infinite contours of the divine substance, or a key to unlock one of the doors in the house with many mansions. For it is not humanity that is to be saved, but you—you, the individual reader. . . . Blessed and fortunate creature, your eyes shall behold him, your eyes and not another's. All that you are, sins apart, is destined, if you will let God have his way, to utter satisfaction. . . . Your place in heaven will seem to be made for you and you alone, because you were made for it.[7]

Chesterton wrote about the awkwardness of seeking to do justice to earthly existence—of "loving the world without trusting it"—while being haunted by the hound of heaven, saying that all the optimism of his own day was in the end a false optimism, for it was predicated on the idea that man really does fit in to this world, that he really does belong here. But true, Christian optimism says no such thing: "The Christian optimism is based on the fact that we do *not* fit in to the world. I had tried to be happy by telling myself that man is an animal, like any other which sought its meat from God. But now I really was happy, for I had learnt that man is a monstrosity. I had been right in feeling all things as odd, for I myself was at once worse and better than all things."[8] In his own characteristically paradoxical way, Chesterton is saying that as long as he believed that man is nothing more than an animal with no eternal destiny to await or burdensome moral responsibilities to fulfill, he simply could not experience the relief that such a worldview was intended to convey. But once he understood that man is not a mere mammal but a monstrosity, not a beast but a broken god, he

---

6. Shea, *Mary,* 147–48, 181.
7. Lewis, *The Problem of Pain,* quoted in *The Quotable Lewis,* 281–82.
8. Chesterton, *Orthodoxy,* 116, emphasis original.

finally was able to rejoice over the sheer dignity that such an insult implied. After all, calling someone a sinner is an ironic compliment of the highest order, for it means that he is acting beneath his true station, selling himself short, and potentially squandering the royal inheritance for which he was designed. "The modern philosopher had told me again and again that I was in the right place, and I had still felt depressed even in acquiescence. But I had heard that I was in the *wrong* place, and my soul sang for joy, like a bird in spring. The knowledge found out and illuminated forgotten chambers in the dark house of infancy. I knew now why grass had always seemed to me as queer as the green beard of a giant, and why I could feel homesick at home."[9] Simply put, the Christian faith alone is able to make sense out of the complexity of human life, for in Christ and in his Church is found the fulfillment of everything good, and true, and beautiful about the world. Jesus comes to the world "not with the destructive force of a battering ram, but with the effectiveness of a key," for the gospel's job is not to un*do*, but to un*lock*.[10] And make no mistake, Christianity is for this reason quite complex, but that is because keys need to be in order to actually work, in order to properly fit the keyhole: "When once one believes in a creed, one is proud of its complexity, as scientists are proud of the complexity of science. It shows how rich it is in discoveries. If it is right at all, it is a compliment to say that it's elaborately right. A stick might fit a hole or a stone a hollow by accident. But a key and a lock are both complex. And if a key fits a lock, you know it is the right key."[11]

Returning to what we said earlier about telling the truth versus lying, while it may make us feel better to be told that man is simple enough to be defined by our animal instincts that make us desire food, water, and sex, such a description is akin to looking at a peacock's tail and calling it "blue." Sure, there is blue in it, but the spectrum of colors represented is much more rich and complex than that. In fact, reducing man to merely what he shares in common with animals does not free him to love, but consigns him to self-preservation. "For if we act as though we come from chaos," writes Shea, "we inevitably return to chaos. If we insist there's no outside beyond nature, no transcendent God by whom we are made and to whom we shall return, then we murder each other by the millions to get the biggest piece

9. Ibid., emphasis original.
10. Fagerberg, *The Size of Chesterton's Catholicism*, 109.
11. Chesterton, *Orthodoxy*, 120.

of the pie here and now. For, as Dostoyevsky's Ivan Karamazov said, 'If there is no God, everything is permissible.'"[12] Shea continues:

> And so, as the nineteenth century attacked the dignity of our origins in unprecedented ways, the twentieth century blasphemed (and the twenty-first century continues to blaspheme) the dignity of our *destiny*. Again and again and again, the twentieth century screamed and blared that our final destiny was the oven, the mass grave, the concentration camp, the gas chamber, the muddy trench, the frozen Siberian waste, the anonymity of the cubicle, the facelessness of the production line, the dereliction of the nursing home, the dumpster behind the abortuary. It taught us that people who can't produce should die; people with defective bodies or brains should die; people who did not look like us should die; children should die; old people should die; and that we are all means to ends and not creatures made in the image of God, for whom he was willing to die.[13]

Life, like the peacock's hue, is complex and therefore needs to be considered through a lens that refuses to be reductionistic or to limit our options to just black and white (or blue). It is the Christian faith that provides this lens through which the beautiful and ornate complexity of human existence can be appreciated, providing us (to mix my metaphors) a framework upon which all the things we know to be true about the world can be hung.

> I had found this hole in the world: the fact that one must somehow find a way of loving the world without trusting it; somehow one must love the world without being worldly. I found this projecting feature of Christian theology, like a sort of hard spike, the dogmatic insistence that God was personal, and had made a world separate from Himself. The spike of dogma fitted exactly the hole in the world—it had evidently been meant to go there—and then the strange thing began to happen. When once these two parts of the two machines had come together, one after another, all the other parts fitted and fell in with an eerie exactitude.

"Instinct after instinct," concludes Chesterton, "was answered by doctrine after doctrine."[14]

It is precisely because the natural world bears witness to all the good things that Christianity fulfills that nature and grace need not be at war,

---

12. Shea, *Mary*, 176–77.
13. Ibid., 177, emphasis original.
14. Chesterton, *Orthodoxy*, 114–15.

The Destiny of the Species

and the earthliness of our origin need not preclude the heavenliness of our destiny. But according to the closed system of Darwinian theory, nature is our Mother and we are confined to a one-parent home. Yet as Chesterton points out, if nature is our Mother, she is at best a Stepmother. Christianity, on the other hand, insists that "nature is not our mother: Nature is our sister. We can be proud of her beauty, since we have the same Father; but she has no authority over us; we have to admire, but not to imitate." If Lewis was right when he said that if we aim at heaven we get earth thrown in for free, then we can be liberated to follow Chesterton's urging and look at the natural world as a sister, "and even a younger sister: a little, dancing sister, to be laughed at as well as loved."[15]

This present age, when recognized as penultimate rather than ultimate, can thence be enjoyed when enjoyable, endured when uncomfortable, and suffered through when torturous, all because it need not bear the burden of being the destiny of the species. For that, we look beyond this vale of tears to the age to come, to the New Jerusalem, and to the eternal city whose Builder and Maker is God (Heb. 11:10).

---

15. Ibid., 167.

Bibliography

Anselm, *Proslogium; Monologium; An Appendix in Behalf of The Fool by Gaunilon; and Cur Deus Homo.* La Salle: The Open Court Publishing Company, 1951.
Berry, Wendell, *The Art of the Commonplace.* Berkeley: Counterpoint Press, 2002.
Bono, *The Book of Psalms.* New York: Grove Press, 1999.
Brooks, David, *On Paradise Drive: How We Live Now (And Always Have) in the Future Tense.* New York: Simon and Schuster, 2004.
Chesterton, G.K., *Orthodoxy.* Colorado Springs: WaterBrook Press, 2001.
——— *What's Wrong with the World.* McLean, VA: IndyPublish.com.
Dark, David, *Everyday Apocalypse: The Sacred Revealed in Radiohead, The Simpsons and Other Pop Culture Icons.* Grand Rapids: Brazos Press, 2002.
Fagerberg, David W., *The Size of Chesterton's Catholicism.* Notre Dame: University of Notre Dame Press, 1998.
Klein, Naomi, *No Logo.* New York: Picador, 2000.
Kreeft, Peter, *Heaven: The Heart's Greatest Longing.* San Francisco: Ignatius Press, 1989.
——— *Three Philosophies of Life.* San Francisco: Ignatius Press, 1989.
——— http://www.peterkreeft.com/topics/heaven.htm
Lewis, C.S., *The Quotable Lewis*, Martindale and Root, eds. Wheaton: Tyndale House Publications, 1989.
———*A Year with C.S. Lewis* (San Francisco: HarperSanFrancisco, 2003.
Loy, David, "Religion and the Market," *Journal of the American Association of Religion* , 1997.
Manning, Brennan, *The Ragamuffin Gospel.* Portland: Multnomah, 1990.
Merton, Thomas, *Seeds.* Boston: Shambhala Publications, 2002.
Niebuhr, H. Richard, *The Kingdom of God in America.* New York: Harper and Row, 1959.
Schor, Juliet, *The Overspent American: Why We Want What We Don't Need.* New York: HarperCollins Publishers, 1998.
Shea, Mark, *Mary, Mother of the Son II, First Guardian of the Faith.* San Diego: Catholic Answers, 2009.
Sirota, David, *The Uprising: An Unauthorized Tour of the Populist Revolt Scaring Wall Street and Washington.* New York: Crown Publishers, 2008.
Stellman, Jason J., *Dual Citizens: Worship and Life between the Already and Not Yet* . Lake Mary, FL: Reformation Trust, 2009.
Stiles, Paul, *Is the American Dream Killing You?: How "The Market" Rules Our Lives.* New York: HarperCollins Publishers, 2005.

Bibliography

Taibbi, Matt, *The Great Derangement: A Terrifying True Story of War, Politics, and Religion*. New York: Spiegel and Grau, 2008.

Wright, J. Lenore, "Sam and Frodo's Excellent Adventure: Tolkien's Journey Motif" in Gregory Bassham and Eric Bronson (eds.) *The Lord of the Rings and Philosophy*. Chicago: Carus Publishing Company, 2003.

Wright, N.T., *The Climax of the Covenant*. Minneapolis: Fortress Press, 1993.

www.ingramcontent.com/pod-product-compliance
Lightning Source LLC
Chambersburg PA
CBHW070924160426
43193CB00011B/1569